ROUTLEDGE LIBRARY EDITIONS:
THE ECONOMY OF THE MIDDLE EAST

Volume 27

THE ROLE OF GOVERNMENT IN THE INDUSTRIALIZATION OF IRAQ 1950–1965

THE ROLE OF GOVERNMENT IN THE INDUSTRIALIZATION OF IRAQ 1950–1965

FERHANG JALAL

LONDON AND NEW YORK

First published in 1972

This edition first published in 2014
by Routledge
2 Park Square, Milton Park, Abingdon, Oxon, OX14 4RN

and by Routledge
711 Third Avenue, New York, NY 10017

Routledge is an imprint of the Taylor & Francis Group, an informa business

© 1972 F. Jalal

All rights reserved. No part of this book may be reprinted or reproduced or utilised in any form or by any electronic, mechanical, or other means, now known or hereafter invented, including photocopying and recording, or in any information storage or retrieval system, without permission in writing from the publishers.

Trademark notice: Product or corporate names may be trademarks or registered trademarks, and are used only for identification and explanation without intent to infringe.

British Library Cataloguing in Publication Data
A catalogue record for this book is available from the British Library

ISBN: 978-1-138-78710-0 (Set)
eISBN: 978-1-315-74408-7 (Set)
ISBN: 978-1-138-81547-6 (Volume 27)
eISBN: 978-1-315-74445-2 (Volume 27)
Pb ISBN: 978-1-138-82030-2 (Volume 27)

Publisher's Note
The publisher has gone to great lengths to ensure the quality of this reprint but points out that some imperfections in the original copies may be apparent.

Disclaimer
The publisher has made every effort to trace copyright holders and would welcome correspondence from those they have been unable to trace.

THE ROLE OF GOVERNMENT IN THE INDUSTRIALIZATION OF IRAQ 1950–1965

Dr. Ferhang Jalal

FRANK CASS : LONDON

First Published in 1972 by

FRANK CASS AND COMPANY LIMITED

67 Great Russell Street, London, WC1B 3BT

Distributed in the United States by

International Scholarly Book Services, Inc.

Beaverton, Oregon 97005

Library of Congress Catalog Card Number 77-171260

ISBN 0 7146 2586 8

Copyright © 1972 F. JALAL

All Rights Reserved. No part of this publication may be repro-duced in any form or by any means, electronic, mechanical, photocopying, recording or otherwise, without the prior permis-sion of Frank Cass and Company Limited in writing.

Printed in Great Britain by

The Whitefriars Press, London and Tonbridge

Contents

	Page
List of Tables	vii
Preface	xi

I *Government and Economic Development: 1920–50*
1 Conditions in 1920 ... 1
2 Government Development Effort 1921–50 ... 3
3 Conditions in 1950 ... 7
4 Main Problems of Development ... 10

II *The Organization and Administration of Government Investment Programmes: 1950–65*
1 The Development Board 1950–58 ... 14
2 The Planning Board 1959–65 ... 19
3 The Ministry of Industry ... 21
4 Administrative Defects ... 27

III *Formulation of Government Investment Programmes: 1951–65*
1 Plans of the Development Board ... 32
2 Plans of the Planning Board ... 38
3 Size of Plans ... 42
4 The Sectoral Allocation ... 44
5 The Choice of Projects ... 53

IV *Implementation of Government Investment Programmes: 1951–65*
1 The Experience of Implementation ... 62
2 The Main Causes of Failure ... 69

V *Financial Institutions and Industrialization*
1 Commercial Banks and the Finance of Industry ... 80
2 The Industrial Bank ... 88

VI Other Policies to Promote Industrialization
1	Protection	102
2	Tax Exemption	119
3	The Licensing of Industrial Enterprises	122

VII Summary and Conclusions 127

Bibliography 135

Index 141

List of Tables

Table No.		Page
I.1	Authorized Expenditure under Capital Budgets 1931–42	4
I.2	Average Government Capital Expenditure and Current Expenditure Compared with Average Gross Capital Formation, Oil Royalties, Government Revenues and Value of Exports 1921–50	5
I.3	Allocation of Funds between Major Sectors in the 1934–38 and 1949–53 Government Capital Budgets	6
I.4	Average Gross Investment by Major Sectors 1933–50	6
I.5	A Comparison between Some Aspects of Iraq's Conditions in 1920 and 1950	9
I.6	Oil Revenue compared to Total Government Revenues, Government Capital Expenditure and Value of other Exports 1951–65	11
III.1	Plans of the Development Board 1951–60	33
III.2	The Industrial Sector of the Second Plan 1955–59	35
III.3	The Industrial Sector of the Third Plan 1955–60	37
III.4	Projects Suggested by the Little Report and included in the Third Plan	38
III.5	Investment Programmes of the Planning Board 1959–65	38
III.6	The Industrial Sector of the Fourth Plan 1959–62	40
III.7	The Industrial Sector of the Fifth Plan 1961–65	40
III.8	The Industrial Sector of the Sixth Plan 1965–69	41
III.9	Investment Requirements of the Five-Year Plan 1965–69	45
III.10	Planned Distribution of Funds among Different Sectors 1951–65	47
III.11	Growth of Industrial Branches Derived from the U.N. Pattern of Industrial Growth Technique	55
III.12	Priority Ratios in the Sixth Plan 1965–69: The Industrial Sector—Selected Projects	58
IV.1	Planned Investment, Actual Capital Expenditure, and Total Revenues of the Development Programmes 1951–65	63
IV.2	Actual Expenditure by Sectors as % of Annual Sectoral Allocation 1951–65	65
IV.3	Sectoral Distribution of Planned Investment 1951–65	66

viii LIST OF TABLES

IV.4	Sectoral Actual Investment as % of Total Investment 1951–65	67
IV.5	Deviation of Actual Pattern of Expenditure from Planned Composition of Investment 1951–65	68
IV.6	Distribution of Actual Revenue between Sectors according to Priorities of the 1959–65 Plan	70
IV.7	Overestimated Revenues and the Deviation of the Actual Pattern of Investment from the Planned Pattern 1959–65	71
IV.8	A comparison between Government Capital Expenditure, Current Expenditure and National Income 1951–65	72
IV.9	Main elements of Government Ordinary Budget Expenditure 1951–65	74
IV.10	Administrative Expenditure, Planned Investment and Actual Capital Expenditure in the Building Sector and the Industrial Sector 1959–63	76
V.1	The Ratio of Working Capital to Fixed Capital in Thirty Major Industrial Companies 1962	82
V.2	Consolidated Balance Sheet of Thirty Major Industrial Companies 1962	83
V.3	Consolidated Balance Sheet, Liquidity Ratios and Excess Reserves of Iraq's Commercial Banks	85
V.4	Volume, Withdrawals and Velocity of Circulation of Demand, Time and Saving Deposits of the Private Sector with Iraq's Commercial Bank 1952–65	87
V.5	Resources of the Industrial Bank 1950–65	90
V.6	Sources of Revenue of the Industrial Bank 1950–65	91
V.7	Number and Amount of Long and Medium Term Loans by the Industrial Bank 1950–65	92
V.8	Distribution of Loans made by the Industrial Bank According to their Size 1961–65	93
V.9	Number and Value of Loans by the Industrial Bank According to Maturity 1965	95
V.10	Value of Short-term Loans Advanced by the Industrial Bank 1950–65	95
V.11	Number of Companies in which the Industrial Bank Participated and the Value of its Shares	97
V.12	Companies in which the Industrial Bank was a Shareholder in July 1964	97
V.13	The Industrial Bank's Participation in Industrial Companies, December 1965	98
VI.1	Import Duties as a Source of Government Revenue 1950–65	106

VI.2	Protective Aspects of Tariffs: The Simple and the Refined Average Tariffs 1950–65	108
VI.3	Average Tariff on Selected Imports Competing Commodities 1956 and 1962	110
VI.4	Values of Import Licences and Actual Imports 1950–65	112
VI.5	Imports of Capital Goods 1950–65	114
VI.6	Number of Industrial Products Completely or Partly Protected by Quotas 1960–65	116

Preface

Since 1950 the Government of Iraq has attempted vigorously to develop the economy. In this study I have discussed, analysed and appraised a number of policies adopted by the Government to promote the growth of the industrial sector. The rest of the economy is brought into the picture only to show the relative importance of the industrial sector and to clarify certain aspects of its relations with other sectors. I have used statistics whenever possible, but the study has an institutional bias because I wish to stress the institutional and administrative bottlenecks to industrial development in Iraq. I have concentrated on the period 1950–65, but where the discussion became concerned with the historical development of institutions and polices I have covered a longer time period.

The volume is divided into seven chapters. The first chapter is devoted to the Government's efforts to develop the economy before 1950 and forms a background to the study of the period 1950–65. In Chapter II the Government's attempts to create an organizational system to formulate and implement its industrial plans are discussed. This chapter also analyses the characteristics of Iraq's public administration and describes the internal organization of the Ministry of Industry.

Chapter III deals with investment programmes formulated during 1951–65. In this chapter I discuss the methods of plan formulation, the size of the plans, the allocation of investment among different sectors of the economy and the choice of projects in the industrial sector. In Chapter IV I outline the implementation process for investment programmes. Because of the reorganization of the planning machinery in 1959, and the change in policy after the revolution of July 1958, I divided the chapter into two sub-periods 1950–58 and 1959–65 and have made comparisons between the periods.

Chapter V deals with policy towards institutions concerned with the finances of private industry. In the first part of the chapter the discussion concentrates on the role of commercial banks and the Central Bank of Iraq in providing working capital to industry. In the second part of the chapter I discuss the activities of the Industrial Bank of Iraq, namely its provision of short and long-term loans, its participation in the equity capital of private companies and its efforts to give industry technical assistance. Chapter VI is devoted to the consideration of protection, tax exemption and control over the allocation of private investment in industry. In Chapter VII I summarize the study and offer my conclusions.

The Government has not sought to encourage the growth of industry through a multiple exchange rate policy or through bilateral trade agreements. Nor did it guarantee minimum profits on investment in industry. These policy instruments are therefore not relevant to this study.

I must express my indebtedness to my colleagues in the Iraqi Ministry of Industry and other Departments who have provided me with all published and unpublished material, laws and regulations required for this study. In particular I acknowledge my thanks to Mr. M. H. al-Baya, Mr. M. Said and Mr. S. Atto.

I wish also to thank the Industrial Bank of Iraq, and the British Council who jointly sponsored my scholarship without which it would have been very difficult to undertake this study.

I have had many useful discussions with Dr. A. Kelidar and Mr. R. Mabro. My greatest obligations are however to Professor E. T. Penrose and Dr. P. K. O'Brien for their continuous encouragement and advice in the preparation of this study. For any mistakes made, however, they must not be held responsible.

Finally, my wife has suffered a great deal from my academic ambitions; many thanks to her for her patience.

1970
Baghdad

F. Jalal

Chapter I

GOVERNMENT AND ECONOMIC DEVELOPMENT: 1921–50

The main purpose of this chapter is to show governmental efforts to develop the economy before 1950, as a background to my study during the period 1950–65. This chapter includes a brief description of the economy in 1920, which is compared to conditions of the country in 1950, and shows the slow progress during those three decades. The role of Government in the development of the economy is shown through the analysis of its capital expenditure in comparison to total government expenditure and gross capital formation. Two of the main factors which caused slow progress were shortage of Government revenue and political instability. The vast increase in oil revenues from 1950 solved the first problem. By comparing oil revenue to other sources of government finance, state development expenditure, and exports other than oil, it is possible to show that at that time, the stage was set for a much higher rate of capital formation. It remained for the Government, however, to devise an organization which could provide continuity in development work.

1. Conditions in 1920

Present-day Iraq, which consists mainly, but not entirely of ancient Mesopotamia, became a political entity in 1920. The first Iraqi Government was formed under the British Mandate in 1921 and achieved independence in 1932.[1]

From 1920, the country started simultaneously to build a national administration and to develop its resources. Conditions at that time were such, that its economic development required the provision of basic public services, without which productive activity of all kinds cannot function properly. These include law and order, education and public health, transportation and communication, power and water supply, irrigation, drainage and flood control. This was necessary because during the Ottoman rule in Iraq (1534–1917), public services remained meagre and economic activity was handicapped by lack of social overhead capital. 'For example in 1878, it cost about $1.50 to transport a dollar's worth of grain from Hilla to Baghdad—a distance of about 60 miles',[2] because Iraq's roads were

2 ROLE OF GOVERNMENT IN INDUSTRIALIZATION OF IRAQ

mere tracks suitable only for goods carried by animals. Moreover, the administration outside the large towns was ineffective; hence the need to pay dues to tribes through whose territory goods were transported.[3]

Before the First World War, a small section of a railway was completed by the Ottoman Government, but during the war and immediately after it British occupation forces constructed a railway system which connected Baghdad with Basrah in the south and Khanaqin and Kirkuk in the north-east. This was an important improvement but 'The total length of the railway system was 1,139 miles in 1920 consisting however of a number of unconnected sections built for the most part of second-hand rails . . . and the rolling stock was a heterogeneous collection of such second-hand or worse vehicles as could be spared from the Indian railway.'[4] By 1920, other sorts of mechanized transportation were introduced and there were 3,500 kilometres of roads, but they were all earth roads impassable for a great part of the year by the few dozen motor vehicles operating in the country then.[5]

Public utilities were practically non-existent during the Ottoman rule. Electric generating equipment was never installed and no town had a modern water supply. By 1920 only 'an inefficient installation pumped crude river water into Baghdad, but no other town in the country had either electricity or pumped water'.[6] But the water of the rivers of Iraq 'are high in colloidal and organic materials, and usually high in bacteria. It is necessary, therefore to treat such supplies of water for human consumption if general health is to be maintained'.[7]

The health organization of Iraq during the Turkish rule 'existed largely on paper'.[8] Foreigners visiting the holy shrines in Iraq or on their way to Mecca through the country usually exposed it to dangers of imported epidemic diseases,[9] yet 'quarantine was still largely a bribe-extracting force'.[10] By 1920, there were 51 dispensaries, 25 Iraqi doctors, and 28 hospitals, but only one or two of these deserved the name of hospital.[11]

Education suffered from neglect during the Ottoman rule and the methods of teaching were primitive.[12] In 1920 there were 84 primary schools with 6,742 students and 363 teachers; there were four secondary schools and one college of law with only 65 students. The meagreness of educational facilities is reflected in the fact that almost 98% of the population were illiterate.[13]

Public administration during the Ottoman rule was highly centralized, minute decisions were referred to the next highest authority and often to Constantinople. The administration was undermined by intrigue and a responsible bureaucracy did not

GOVERNMENT AND ECONOMIC DEVELOPMENT 3

develop. Moreover, 'tribal life dominated the countryside and tribal leaders, often at loggerheads with each other were more or less independent of effective Turkish control',[14] yet there is no doubt that an effective control over the whole country and an efficient bureaucracy are necessary for the development of the country. In this respect the country in 1920 was only slightly better, if at all, than it was previously.

The Ottoman regime provided no major water storage, drainage or flood control facilities and widespread flooding continued to be one of Iraq's major problems. It did, however, authorize Sir William Willcocks, a British engineer, to carry out a survey of Iraq's irrigation system. He submitted his recommendations in 1911, and one of his proposals, the Hindiyah Barrage, was completed in 1913, which provided an adequate flow of water through the Hilla branch of the Middle Euphrates and this prevented a large area from going out of cultivation.[15] But in 1920, the Barrage was 'already in a weak condition, a part of the floor and a subsidiary weir downstream of the regulating gates having been destroyed by the action of the river and the original steel gates having proved unsuitable for their purpose'.[16]

Other elements of social overhead capital were in no better condition during the Ottoman rule. For example, before the First World War 'there were no port facilities at Basrah (Iraq's only port) except three custom examination sheds . . . The conditions of loading and unloading were exceedingly primitive.'[17] By 1920 modern port facilities were installed in Basrah which were ample for the demand on their services.[18]

Table I.5 summarizes conditions in the country between 1920 and 1921 and shows how primitive it was, not so very long ago.

2. Government Development Efforts 1921-50

The newly established Government assumed full responsibility for the development of the country, right from 1921. In its development activities, besides the ordinary budgets, it had an extraordinary budget which was part of the former budget and under the control of the Ministry of Finance. The accounts of this budget were devoted to capital works.[19] These capital budgets were in the form of five or four-year programmes, a number of which are summarized in Table I.1. The table shows a rapid change of programmes and the reason behind this will be explained later. Each of these development programmes had a schedule attached to it, specifying on what projects funds were to be spent. But these programmes did not include development projects carried out by semi-autonomous organizations of the Government, such as the Port of

TABLE 1.1

Authorized Expenditure under Capital Budgets
1931–42

	I.D. thousands	
	Total Authorized Expenditure	Average Annual Authorized Expenditure
1931–35	2,210	442
1934–38	3,237	647
1936–40	4,120	824
1938–42	8,230	1,049
1939–42	11,135	2,783

Source: Government of Iraq, Laws No. 79 (1931), No. 39 (1934), No. 33 (1936), No. 45 (1938), No. 37 (1939) and Ordinance No. 28 (1935)
Note: One Iraqi Dinar (I.D.)=1,000 fils=£1 sterling from 1931–65

Basrah Authority and the Railway Administration, which had separate budgets from the Government budget, and each carried out its own development programme.[20]

Table I.2 shows total Government expenditure on capital works compared with total expenditure and gross fixed capital formation. As a percentage of total Government expenditure, capital expenditure rose very rapidly during the 1930s. During the war, development expenditure dropped considerably, both in absolute terms and as a percentage of total expenditure. Although capital expenditure started to rise after the war, it did not recover the pre-war level as a percentage of total expenditure.[21] In absolute terms, capital expenditure was greater in the post-war years than in the pre-war period, but did not return to the pre-war level of I.D. 2.4 million per annum during 1936–40,[22] in real terms, because the purchasing power of the Iraqi Dinar during the post-war period was about a quarter of its pre-war level.[23] Table I.2 shows that the share of Government in gross investment was 34% during 1921–50. Its share, however, was rising before the war and the Government was responsible for 68% of gross investment during 1936–40, but its share declined to 26% during 1946–50.[24]

The investment by the Government went almost entirely into social overhead capital; there was no direct Government investment in the manufacturing sector. Projects included in these investment programmes were: Government administrative buildings, schools, hospitals, clinics, quarantine stations, museums, resort hotels, roads, bridges, wireless, telephone and telegraph lines, barrages, canals, etc. Of special interest to our study is the fact that

TABLE I.2

Average Government Capital Expenditure and Current Expenditure Compared with Average Gross Capital Formation, Oil Royalties, Government Revenues and Value of Exports 1921–50

I.D. Millions

	Total Govmt. Revenue 1	Oil Revenue 2	Ord. Expend. 3	Capital Expend. 4	3 + 4 5	Gross Cap. Formtn. 6	Export other than Oil 7	2 + 7 8	2 as % of 1 9	2 as % of 8 10	4 as % of 5 11	4 as % of 6 12
1921–25	3·9	0	3·7	0	3·7	0·6	3·5	3·5	0	0	0	0
1926–30	4·1	0	4·2	0·1	4·3	1·3	3·8	3·8	0	0	0·2	8
1931–35	4·2	0·7	3·8	0·5	4·3	1·6	2·6	3·3	17	21·2	11·6	31
1936–40	7·6	1·6	5·8	2·4	8·2	3·5	3·9	5·5	21	29·1	29·2	68
1941–45	16·2	2·0	14·1	1·1	15·2	2·7	7·2	9·2	12	21·7	7·2	41
1946–50	27·9	3·4	25·1	3·5	28·6	13·6	12·0	15·4	12	22·1	12·2	26
									15	19·0	12·0	34

Source: Ministry of Finance Department of Accounts, *Annual Report*, 1959, p. 61; Ministry of Planning, Central Bureau of Statistics, *Summary of Iraq Foreign Trade 1927–60*, pp. 2–3; Hassan, *Economic Development of Iraq*, p. 534; al-Atraqchi, *Pattern of Foreign Trade of Iraq 1948–62*, pp. 106, 296; Jamil, *Commercial Policy of Iraq*, pp. 68, 72, 211, 402 and Abu-El-Haj, *Capital Formation in Iraq*, 1921–57, p. 4

Note: Dr. Abu-El-Haj's figures for capital formation during 1921–45 did not include private expenditure on buildings. On the basis of his figures the share of this type of expenditure was 25% of gross capital expenditure. I have adjusted 1921–45 figures by adding 25% to make the series comparable, for these are the only available estimates of capital formation during that period.

6 ROLE OF GOVERNMENT IN INDUSTRIALIZATION OF IRAQ

these programmes provided for the establishment of a refinery and the Agricultural-Industrial Bank, but in fact the direct contribution of these programmes to the industrial sector was the provision of funds for the Bank, which started operation in 1936.[25] The concentration of Government capital expenditure on social overhead capital is clear from Table I.3 which summarizes the schedules attached to the 1934–38 and 1949–53 programmes. Out of I.D. 108,000 allocated for other purposes, I.D. 65,000, or 2% of total allocations, was devoted in the 1934–38 programme to the establishment of state industrial projects and the encouragement of private industries. The Government did not invest directly in the manufacturing sector, and this is one of the reasons why the share of industry in total investment was low, as can be seen from Table I.4.

To comprehend the magnitude of capital formation, it would be useful to compare it with national income, but unfortunately estimates for the period are not available. The national income of Iraq, in 1949, was estimated at roughly I.D. 140 million.[26] Since total gross investment during the same year was I.D. 14 million,[27] gross

TABLE I.3

Allocation of Funds between Major Sectors in the 1934–38 and 1949–53 Government Capital Budgets

	I.D. Thousands			
Major Sector	*1934–38*		*1949–53*	
	I.D.	%	*I.D.*	%
Irrigation	1,891	58·5	35,300	61
Building	943	29·1	11,600	20
Communication	293	9·0	9,000	17
Other	108	3·4	1,000	2

Source: Government of Iraq, Law No. 39 (1934) and Langley, *Industrialization of Iraq*, p. 167

TABLE I.4

Average Gross Investment by Major Sectors 1933–50

	I.D. Thousands				
	Agriculture	*Transporta-tion*	*Industry*	*Others*	*Total*
1933–39	520	1,300	120	420	2,360
1946–50	2,000	5,500	570	2,860	10,930
	Percent of Total				
1933–39	22%	55%	5%	18%	100%
1946–50	19%	50%	5%	26%	100%

Source: Abu-El-Haj, *Capital Formation in Iraq, 1921–57*, p. 10

GOVERNMENT AND ECONOMIC DEVELOPMENT

investment was roughly 10% of national income in 1949. On the other hand, Dr. Fenelon estimated that gross domestic investment was 11% of gross national product in 1950.[28] So far as these figures represent the period under study, the ratio of gross investment to national income seems to have been around 10%. Although the Government's share of investment expenditure was high, the share of investment in gross national product was relatively low. Moreover, the level of national income was extremely low. Therefor the investable funds under the control of the Government were small in magnitude. These funds were not enough to support large development programmes or even one large flood control complex, necessary to control the exceptionally difficult environment of Iraq and to make possible a rapid utilization of the country's water resources. For example, total Government expenditure on capital formation during the period 1941–49 was less than the total cost of building the Thartar-Habaniya flood control complex.[29] Given the desperate need for all kinds of social overhead capital, the available funds, over and above the ordinary government expenditure, were fully utilized to finance the most necessary investment in social overhead capital. Under these circumstances, the Government could not implement a policy of industrialization based on direct government investment. The reason for the absence of direct investment in this sector was not the unwillingness of the Government to enter the industrial sectors, but basically the lack of means to finance industrialization.

3. *Conditions in 1950*

Unfortunately the financial resources of the Government were only sufficient to allow a very moderate expansion of social overhead capital, thus, although the framework of the required facilities was laid down, most of them were still in poor condition in the early 1950s and in need of substantial expansion, despite the fact that, compared with 1920, important progress had been achieved. For example, the length of the road system increased from 3,500 kilometres in 1920, to 8,000 kilometres in 1950,[30] and this included 2,500 kilometres of metalled and surfaced and 500 kilometres of metalled roads. But the road system was nevertheless in a poor condition and impassable in most places for a large part of the year.[31] In 1950, a programme was laid down for building and improving 37 major roads with a total length of 3,463 kilometres, which was a sound programme according to the I.B.R.D. Mission's Report. The Mission pointed out that in addition 'agricultural and forestry development areas need feeder roads to the nearest railway station or main road or both . . . to the length of 8,000 kilometres'.[32]

8 ROLE OF GOVERNMENT IN INDUSTRIALIZATION OF IRAQ

The Mission found that the railway system, which consisted at that time of a single line of metre gauge linking up the north-east with the south, through Baghdad, and another standard gauge single line which connected Baghdad with Mosul and the Syrian border, was on the whole ample for the demand at the time. It nevertheless agreed more or less with the recommendations of the consulting engineers, Rendal, Palmer & Tritton, of Westminster, London, who, in 1951, recommended a detailed rehabilitation and modernization programme for the railway system. Moreover, the Mission maintained that there was 'no doubt that the division of the railway system into two gauges with a trans-shipment point in the centre [was] a handicap to full traffic development'.[33] Adding to this the expected increase in demand, which was such that the system was operating at full capacity by 1956,[34] meant that expansion was clearly needed in the railway system. This, together with the Basrah Port facilities, provided the most advanced capital infrastructure in Iraq at that time.

Table 1.5 shows that during the three decades the numbers of schools, teachers, pupils, colleges etc., increased vastly. Nevertheless, in 1950, there were 175,000 children in schools out of about 750,000 of school age and probably 87% of the population was illiterate.[35] Despite considerable progress in the health services which is clear from Table I.5, as a result of which the incidence of epidemics was cut down, there was need for much further progress because 'the main endemic diseases—malaria, schistosomiasis, trachoma and ankylostomiasis [were] still very common'.[36]

Infant mortality was estimated to be 250 per thousand live births and 'about 20% of the young men liable for military service [were] found to be unfit due to diseases that affect their ability to work.'[37] A safe water supply is one of the keys to the health problem; by 1950, 40 municipalities had modern safe water supplies, but this was not enough and a plan was prepared to provide 114 municipalities having a total population of 950,000 with these facilities. The World Bank Mission found that the programme was sound and stated that 'there are numerous villages in addition to municipalities where the problem of obtaining water is critical',[38] hence the need for a much larger programme. Considerable progress was achieved in providing large towns with electricity. Nevertheless a large number of municipalities had no electricity at all; moreover, per capita consumption of power in Iraq was among the lowest in the world and power rates among the highest.[39] Sewage was completely neglected, even in Baghdad, but post, telegraphs, radio communications, air transport and city transport were all established but all in need of further drastic expansion.[40]

GOVERNMENT AND ECONOMIC DEVELOPMENT 9

TABLE I.5

A Comparison between Some Aspects of Iraq's Conditions in 1920 and 1950

	Unit	1920–21	1949–50
Length of the Railway System	L	1,339	1,648
Length of the Road System	,,	3,500	8,000
Metalled and Surfaced	,,		2,500
Metalled only	,,		500
Earth Roads	,,	3,500	5,000
Government Primary Schools	No.	84	1,100
Pupils in Government Primary Schools	,,	6,742	175,000
Teachers in Primary Schools	,,	363	6,588
Government Secondary Schools	,,	4	108
Pupils in Secondary Schools	,,	233	19,453
Teachers in Secondary Schools	,,	n.a.	871
Colleges	,,	1	9
Pupils in Colleges	,,	65	3,021
Hospitals	,,	28	89
Dispensaries	,,	51	448
Iraqi Doctors	,,	25	797
Towns with Piped Water Supply	,,	1	40
Population	,,	2,840,000	5,000,000
% of Population Illiterate	,,	98%	87%
Towns with Sewage Systems	,,	0	0

Source: Colonial Office, *Progress of Iraq, 1920–31*, pp. 65, 137, 139, 157, 224; I.B.R.D., *Economic Development of Iraq*, pp. 63, 314, 327; Ministry of Education, *Report on Education*, 1949–50 and Ministry of Economy, *Statistical Abstract*, 1951, pp. 87, 98

Note: n.a. means not available

In the field of flood control and irrigation, small works of immediate value such as canals, regulators, and vital flood banks were constructed but 'in the spring disastrous floods often inundate large areas; and in the fall, water was acutely short. Agriculture was hampered not only by the inadequate and irregular supply of water but also by the progressive salination of the soil in the irrigated area'.[41] The extension of flow irrigation, made possible by building the Kut barrage, which was completed in 1939, was an important achievement.[42]

In 1920, aside 'from handicrafts and some cottage industry there was no other industry worth mentioning. Factories were virtually unknown'.[43] But in 1950, the I.B.R.D. Mission reported that 'industry is little developed. Although perhaps as many as 60,000 people are engaged in industrial production (other than oil), virtually all of these are employed in small undertakings where the work is done largely by hand and productivity is accordingly quite low. Probably about 2,000 are working in what might be characterized as modern industrial plants.'[44]

Perhaps the most important single achievement was the extension

10 ROLE OF GOVERNMENT IN INDUSTRIALIZATION OF IRAQ

of the administration to cover the whole country. Thus 'whereas the Turkish Government had exercised rarely more than a partial control, never at one time operative over the whole country, and the Iraqi Government in its early years could claim a wider but still not pervasive authority, in 1950 no surviving enclaves of non-government remained in desert or marsh or mountain'.[45] Nevertheless, the deep roots of instability were still there, mainly because the country was 'still engaged in the process of welding diverse racial and religious groups into conscious nationhood',[46] and 'a formidable range of unsolved problems, inter-Arab and international, political and financial confronted the Government'.[47]

4. *Main Problems of Development*

From the establishment of the Iraqi Government in 1921 until 1950, the country registered slow but appreciable progress. There were many reasons for this slow progress, including lack of state revenue and political instability.

During the period 1921–50, Government revenues were small in relation to ordinary expenditure. It managed, however, to spend, on average, 12% of these revenues on capital works. The ratio of capital expenditure to total Government expenditure was high (29%) during 1935–40. Oil revenues were not large but they were still important, for they represented 15% of total Government revenues during 1931–50, and were equal to 26% of exports other than oil.[48]

A spectacular development in the oil industry in the early 1950s, transformed the prospects of Iraq: oil revenues increased to an extent which made capital cease to be, for all practical purposes, a constraint for many years on the feasible expansion of the economy. Production of oil increased vastly, and according to an agreement between the Government and oil companies, which became effective from the 1st January 1951, they undertook to pay to the Government 50% of the profits attributed to their operation in Iraq. Moreover, the companies guaranteed that the Government's share would not be less than I.D. 20 millions during 1953 and 1954, and not less than I.D. 25 millions in 1955 and annually thereafter. But if prevented by circumstances beyond their control from producing specified quantities, the guaranteed minimum payment would be reduced.[49] Although actual revenues far exceeded these limits, the point is that the Government was sure to receive large and increasing oil revenues. These funds are almost all in foreign exchange. Moreover, they accrue suddenly in large amounts like a windfall which requires virtually no effort; they are like free unconditional foreign aid which amounts to almost a quarter of Iraq's annual

GOVERNMENT AND ECONOMIC DEVELOPMENT 11

national income. Table I.6 brings out the importance of oil revenues. As a source of public revenue they represented almost 60% of total Government revenues; they were the main source of development expenditure and they represented 83% of the country's foreign exchange earnings.

The other major cause of slow progress was lack of continuity in development programmes engendered by political instability. Implementation of development programmes is, by necessity, a long-term task. Continuity requires 'a measure of public tranquility and national cohesion both of which were absent. The period was one of turmoil during which the attention of both the public and the

TABLE I.6

Oil Revenues compared to Total Government Revenues, Capital Expenditure and Value of Other Exports, 1951–65

	I.D. Millions						
	Total Govnmt. Revenue	*Oil Revenue*	*Govnmt. Capital Expend.*	*Non Oil Exports*	$\frac{2}{4}$	*as % of 1*	*as % of 5*
Year	1	2	3	4	5	6	7
1951	44·9	13·9	3·1	27·0	40·9	39·9	44
1952	74·4	40·1	7·8	18·7	58·8	53·8	74
1953	82·9	58·3	12·2	19·0	77·3	70·3	83
1954	97·8	64·3	20·8	17·9	82·2	69·2	93
1955	125·9	73·7	31·3	15·9	89·6	58·5	82
1956	113·8	68·8	43·0	13·1	81·9	60·4	84
1957	97·6	48·8	57·4	12·8	61·6	50·0	79
1958	137·2	79·8	52·2	14·2	94·0	58·2	85
1959	133·2	86·6	49·8	11·4	98·0	65·0	88
1960	151·2	95·1	47·5	7·9	103·0	62·8	92
1961	187·7	94·1	66·9	7·8	101·9	50·5	92
1962	184·7	95·1	58·7	19·3	114·4	51·4	83
1963	194·3	110·0	53·5	16·7	126·7	56·7	87
1964	221·0	126·0	52·1	15·2	141·2	60·2	89
1965	254·0	134·0	57·1	18·1	152·1	54·6	88

Source: Iraq Petroleum Co., *Report on Operation of Oil Companies*, pp. 9, 13; Central Bank of Iraq, *Quarterly Bulletin*, No. 59, p. 32 and *Bulletin New Series*, No. 1, 1965, pp. 30, 33, 61, and No. 4, 1967, pp. 24–7

Government was focussed on political problems . . . The Government was almost continually preoccupied with maintaining its own positions.'[50] Moreover, there was an unusually rapid change of capital expenditure programmes because of the diversity of the views of different Cabinets on how the available funds should be spent.[51] Thus each Cabinet which came to power tried to change the programme of the previous Cabinet and prepared its own programme to be changed by the succeeding Cabinet, if it had time to do that. The reason for rapid Cabinet changes is to be found in the

12 ROLE OF GOVERNMENT IN INDUSTRIALIZATION OF IRAQ

political system. In theory, the Government of Iraq was 'constitutional, representative and democratic',[52] modelled on the British system. In practice the country had what Longrigg called a 'Cabinet Government'.[53] The King chose the Prime Minister; they then together chose members of the Cabinet, on a personal basis, from a group of people constituting a ruling class which 'did not contain a personality capable of single rule, or a group of capable and acceptable oligarchy'.[54] It nevertheless 'contained on the one hand more than enough figures capable of filling the ministerial posts available, but on the other too little variety of viewpoint to compete for power by the advocacy of genuinely alternative programmes. The result was an uneasy shuffle of offices, short-lived Cabinets with a brief innings for everybody'.[55]

Elections were controlled by the Government and frequent dissolutions of Parliament rendered it completely at the mercy of the Cabinet; Parliament was incapable of passing a vote of no confidence in any of the 47 Cabinets during 1921–50. These fell because of internal quarrels, deadlocks, royal disfavour, tribal disorder, public demonstrations and riots, intrigue and military coups d'état, but never through a parliamentary vote of no confidence.[56] By 1950, according to Longrigg, 'internal politics showed no sign of rising above the habitual strife of rival personalities',[57] and it was 'difficult not to anticipate that Cabinet Government would long continue, and with it the rootless precariousness of a regime which seemingly at any time a successful intrigue or a military coup d'état could subvert'.[58]

Under these circumstances it was essential to devise a planning organization and administration which could provide continuity of development work and protect it, as far as possible, from the consequences of rapid Cabinet changes. In the next chapter the attempts of the Government to establish such an organization are discussed.

REFERENCES

1. Khadduri, *Independent Iraq 1932–58*, pp. 1 and 14
2. Geary, *Through Asiatic Turkey*, Vol. 1, p. 190. Quoted by Langley, *The Industrialization of Iraq*, p. 105
3. Langley, *The Industrialization of Iraq*, p. 105
4. Colonial Office, *Special Report on the Progress of Iraq, 1920–31*, p. 157
5. *Ibid.*, pp. 137–9
6. *Ibid.*, p. 141
7. International Bank for Reconstruction and Development, *The Economic Development of Iraq*, p. 458
8. Colonial Office, *Special Report on the Progress of Iraq, 1920–31*, p. 64
9. I.B.R.D., *Economic Development of Iraq*, p. 353
10. Longrigg, *Iraq 1900–1950, A Political, Social and Economic History*, p. 53
11. Qubain, *The Reconstruction of Iraq 1950–57*, p. 18

GOVERNMENT AND ECONOMIC DEVELOPMENT

12. Longrigg, *Iraq, 1900–1950*, p. 37
13. Colonial Office, *Special Report on the Progress of Iraq, 1920–31*, p. 224
14. Langley, *Industrialization of Iraq*, p. 9
15. *Ibid.*, p. 134
16. Colonial Office, *Special Report on the Progress of Iraq, 1920–31*, p. 179
17. *Ibid.*, p. 169
18. *Ibid.*, p. 171
19. Qubain, *Reconstruction of Iraq, 1950–57*, p. 19
20. *Ibid.*, p. 20
21. Table I.2, Column 11
22. Table I.2, Column 4
23. Ministry of Economy *Statistical Abstract, 1958*, pp. 122–8, and Central Bank of Iraq, *Bulletin, New Series*, No. 1, 1965, p. 45
24. Table I.2, Column 12
25. The Bank is studied in Chapter V
26. United Nations, *National and Per Capita Income of Seventy Countries*, pp. 14, 22
27. Abu-El-Haj, *Capital Formation in Iraq*, p. 4
28. Fenelon, K. G. *Iraq, National Income and Expenditure 1950–1956.*
29. Total expenditure on the Thartar project, built during 1952–57, was more than I.D. 17 million, *Ministry of Finance, Department of Accounts, Annual Report on Development Board Projects*, 1959, p. 12
30. Table I.5
31. I.B.R.D., *Economic Development of Iraq*, p. 47
32. Ibid., p. 239
33. *Ibid.*, pp. 319, 324
34. Langley, *Industrialization of Iraq*, p. 117
35. I.B.R.D., *Economic Development of Iraq*, pp. 62–3
36. *Ibid.*, p. 351
37. I.B.R.D., *Economic Development of Iraq*, p. 459
38. *Ibid.*, p. 61
39. *Ibid.*, p. 461
40. *Ibid.*, pp. 332–9, 457
41. *Ibid.*, p. 1
42. al-Khalaf, *The Economic, Physical and Human Geography of Iraq*, p. 213
43. Qubain, *Reconstruction of Iraq*, p. 18
44. I.B.R.D., *Economic Development of Iraq*, p. 2
45. Longrigg, *Iraq 1900–1950*, p. 394
46. Clark, *Compulsory Education in Iraq*, p. 18. Quoted by the I.B.R.D., *Economic Development of Iraq*, p. 66
47. Longrigg, *Iraq 1900–1950*, p. 364
48. See Table I.2
49. Iversen, *Monetary Policy in Iraq*, pp. 95–7
50. Qubain, *Reconstruction of Iraq, 1950–57*, p. 22
51. Colonial Office, *Special Report on the Progress of Iraq, 1920–31*, p. 133, and Qubain, *op. cit.*, pp. 22–3
52. Khadduri, *Independent Iraq, 1932–58*, pp. 13–18
53. Longrigg, *Iraq 1900–1950*, p. 395
54. *Ibid.*, p. 223
55. *Ibid.*, p. 224
56. Khadduri, *Independent Iraq, 1932–58*, pp. 288, 365 and Longrigg, *Iraq, 1900–1950*, p. 395
57. Longrigg, *op. cit.*, p. 364
58. *Ibid.*, p. 397

Chapter II

THE ORGANIZATION AND ADMINISTRATION OF GOVERNMENT INVESTMENT PROGRAMMES: 1950–65

The aim of this chapter is to show Government attempts since 1950 to devise an organizational system which would provide continuity in development work and to describe institutions which evolved from these attempts. Special attention will be paid to the administrative machinery for industrialization. This chapter includes a detailed study of the Development Board, which was established in 1950 and a similar study of the Planning Board, which was established in 1959. We also appraise these organizations to show how far Iraq succeeded in establishing an administration compatible with the magnitude of her investment programmes based on financial resources made available from oil exports.

1. *The Development Board, 1950–58*

To increase the rate of capital formation, made possible by increased oil revenues, it was necessary to draw up co-ordinated investment programmes which required an efficient administration to carry them out. Developing countries, however, 'tend, almost by definition to have underdeveloped administrations',[1] Iraq was no exception in this respect. Although the country had some experience in investment projects and programmes the situation differed radically from the earlier period, because oil revenues made it possible to raise capital expenditure to about 10 times the total public capital expenditure per year during the earlier period. Such a rate of expenditure necessitated 'a substantial improvement in the efficiency of public administration'.[2] The World Bank Mission pointed out many defects in the administration, such as excessive centralization, inadequacy of pay scales, low morale, and lack of any sense of participation in constructive work, which badly affected the efficiency of the administration.[3] It also noticed the lack of co-operation and co-ordination of related activities thus 'various ministries concerned with the erection of schools, hospitals, public buildings and bridges generally locate their projects without reference to an overall plan and without consultation with each other'.[4]

ORGANIZATION AND ADMINISTRATION OF GOVERNMENT 15

The question of improving the administration has many aspects. For example, one may ask whether to plan, in the sense of co-ordinating investment projects, and if so to what extent? What shall be the form of the agency responsible for co-ordination: a Cabinet Committee, a committe of experts or a mixed one? Should the central planning agency be located in the office of the Prime Minister, in some existing ministry, in a new ministry, or should it be an autonomous body outside the regular Government administration? Should planning be separated from implementation, etc.? Clearly there were many alternative approaches to improve and expand the administration; experts on development administration, however, differ on these matters but they agree, more or less, that each country 'has to solve its administrative problems in its own way since the administration is a part of the national culture'.[5]

The Government of Iraq at that time noticed that frequent cabinet changes in the past had made long-term programming impossible.[6] To solve these problems, the Government conceived the idea of entrusting the task of development to a separate organization protected from cabinet changes, run principally by experts and capable of undertaking a planned programme of development. Thus according to Law No. 23, 1950, an autonomous agency was established, called the Development Board, under the presidency of the Prime Minister with a membership including the Minister of Finance and six full-time executive members to be appointed by the Council of Ministers for a five-year term which might be prolonged. Among the full-time executive members, three were to be experts, one in finance and economics, one in irrigation and a third in one other field to be prescribed by the Council of Ministers. One of the executive members was to be the Vice-President of the Board, and one of the expert executive members to be the Secretary General, who signed the Board's contracts and executed its decisions. Liaison with the Government was maintained through the Prime Minister and the Minister of Finance.[7]

The 1950 Law diverted to the Board all oil revenues plus funds which the Parliament might devote to it from time to time, and revenues from loans, external or internal, undertaken by the Board or by the Government on its behalf. After the 1950 oil agreement, which greatly increased the oil revenues, the share of the Development Board was reduced to 70% of these revenues, the other 30% going to the ordinary budget,[8] on the grounds that other relevant Government departments ought to be allowed to carry out minor capital works without passing their plans through the Board.

The Board was given the following tasks: (a) to prepare a general economic and financial plan for the development of the resources

16 ROLE OF GOVERNMENT IN INDUSTRIALIZATION OF IRAQ

of Iraq designed to raise the standard of living of her people, (b) to undertake a general survey of the resources of Iraq, and (c) with the approval of Parliament to carry out projects mentioned in the programme in accordance with their decided priority.

To perform its duties, the Board created administrative machinery under its Secretary General to assist it in formulating and implementing development programmes. Since the Board was not a regular Government agency, its employees did not come under the Civil Service Law. Thus it was able to offer fairly high salaries and attracted technicians and specialists of high quality to its technical departments.[9] These departments were:

1. The First Technical Section, for irrigation, flood control, artesian wells and drainage.
2. The Second Technical Section, for roads, bridges and buildings.
3. The Third Technical Section, for industry, mining and electricity.
4. The Fourth Technical Section, for agriculture and forestry.
5. The Fifth Technical Section, for housing.
6. The Department of Summer Resorts and Tourism.
7. The Miri Land Development Commission, to deal with reclamation and distribution of land and the encouragement of small holdings, and
8. A General Administrative Department.[10]

The establishment of the Development Board created certain problems. The Board was a mixed political and non-political organ consisting partly of cabinet ministers and partly of full-time executive members. It could be argued that it would have been more expedient to make the Board a purely administrative institution, consisting entirely of technical experts and charged, like other Government departments, with the implementation of political decisions taken by the Council of Ministers. Cabinet changes, however, made an organization which could provide continuity in development work highly desirable and the Development Board was exactly such an organization. But continuity by itself is not enough, because ministers are responsible to their country for the success or failure of development plans and they can argue that they cannot be held responsible for the activities of an organization which is not under their direct control.

Considerations of continuity require that the Development Board should have real authority and the means by which it can discharge its responsibility. The Act of 1950 provided the Board with

ORGANIZATION AND ADMINISTRATION OF GOVERNMENT 17

real independence. Considerations of Government authority, however, required a closer link with the Government than was provided by that law. The independence of the Development Board was short-lived before it gave way to pressure from the Cabinet in 1953. At that time the new Government argued that the system of the Development Board gave too little authority and too little information to enable the Government to deal with criticisms in Parliament. The two ex-officio members of the Board were in the minority on a Board of eight which took decisions by simple majority vote and they were fully occupied with other affairs so they could not follow development questions as closely as the executive members.[11] Some Iraqis regarded the Board as a strange organization like a Government inside the Government.[12]

Accordingly Law No. 27 of 1953 was enacted which created a Minister of Development, with ex-officio membership of the Board, and a Ministry of Development under his control. The post of Secretary General was abolished and the Technical Sections were transferred to the Ministry of Development and the Minister assumed the functions of the old Secretary General. The Board, however, remained a mixed committee under the chairmanship of the Prime Minister with the membership including the Ministers of Finance and Development and seven full-time executive members one of whom was to be the permanent Vice-Chairman. The Board continued to have its own budget, which was completely separate from the ordinary budget.

A ministry staffed by career personnel and under the direction of a minister was the normal Government department in Iraq. This form of organization ensures full control by the Government. The danger is that the administration may be subjected to excessive fiscal and personnel restrictions and may not have adequate freedom of action. In fact one of the immediate repercussions of the creation of the Ministry of Development was the downgrading of the salaries of Iraqi employees when they were incorporated into the Civil Service. Several members of the staff consequently resigned which resulted in lower efficiency.[13]

The reorganization of 1953, according to Lord Salter 'fundamentally altered the character and authority of the Board'. The authority of the Government was strengthened and for all practical purposes the Board lost its independence because its action became dependent upon agreement with the Minister of Development, who alone had the technical staff to advise on policy and to implement it. Thus although it was the Board which decided the allocation of funds, the Minister of Development could effectively prevent implementation because the machinery for implementation was

18 ROLE OF GOVERNMENT IN INDUSTRIALIZATION OF IRAQ

under his control. Even if the Board and the Minister of Development were in agreement, frequent changes of ministers would nevertheless delay action because new ministers need time to become familiar with the scope of their work.[14]

The Government thus failed to devise a system which would render the independence of the Board compatible with the authority of the Government. The reorganization of 1953 brought back the danger of instability in the development work. But despite 14 cabinet changes during the period 1951–58[15] 'The Board maintained an autonomous and independent status rarely enjoyed by any other Government agency, and was on the whole immune from political influences',[16] because throughout the period Nuri Said was either in power or very influential and this provided a measure of continuity.[17]

To illustrate the Development Board's system of working we will outline below the procedure for the implementation of industrial projects. The Board decided from the beginning not to set up a complete staff of experts but to use consulting firms to undertake the investigations of the industrial projects covered by its industrial programmes.[18] The consulting firms also prepared designs and specifications, supervised construction and the initial operation of new projects. The third technical section, however, was established for industry, mining and electricity, with a minimum number of experts to assist the Board in selecting a consultant for each project it approved, to co-ordinate activities if several consultants were necessary, and to liaise between the Board and consulting firms and between consultants, contractors and government agencies concerned with a project. According to this system, the implementation of a specific project required a preliminary analysis so that the Board could decide whether the project should be studied in detail. If the preliminary study was encouraging, the Board invited a consultant firm to prepare a feasibility study covering markets, availability of raw materials, labour, transportation, water and power supplies, production costs and the economic justification of the project. The Technical Section then submitted its recommendations to the Board on the feasibility study. If the project was economically sound the consulting firm, after the approval of the Board, started to prepare specifications under which tenders for the construction of the project were invited. The Section reviewed these specifications and if approved by the Board, they were issued internationally. After tenders from contractors were received the consultant analysed them and submitted a report to the Board through the Technical Section.

The next stage was the actual construction of a project by a

ORGANIZATION AND ADMINISTRATION OF GOVERNMENT 19

contractor or contractors, chosen by the Board, under the supervision of the consultant. During this stage the technical section assisted the contractors in overcoming such difficulties as slow custom clearances, transportation delays and disputes with local citizens or officials. While construction was going on, the technical section also selected Iraqis for training, in order to run the factory when it was established. The training was either in local schools or abroad but under the supervision of the consultant or contractor, and it included a period of working in similar industrial plants. The next stage was the initial operation of the plant by the contractors under the supervision of the consultant. Finally, the Development Board handed over the plant to the Ministry of Economy for management.[19]

Thus the planning and implementation of Government industrial projects were entrusted to the Development Board and the Ministry of Development. The related administrative staff consisted of a minimum number of experts; foreign consultants and contractors were used heavily. The Board, however, was not only engaged in general policy but also in the detailed planning and implementation of projects including their detailed technical specifications. In fact nothing was done without the approval of the Board, even the selection of students to be sent abroad for training with respect to the Board's projects. The result was, according to Lord Salter, excessive centralization in the sense of lack of delegation of administrative and detailed planning duties to subordinates and other Government agencies. He noticed that the Board was spending on capital works large sums of money which were nearly as great as the whole ordinary state budget. Most capital works took several years to construct and the administrative work involved was clearly enormous. Lord Salter, therefore, strongly urged that the Development Board 'should as soon and as far as possible be divested both of continuing administrative duties and of the responsibility for detailed as distinct from general planning'.[20]

2. The Planning Board, 1959-65

The Revolution of July 1958 brought, among other things, changes in the Government's development administration. The Development Board was disbanded but the Ministry of Development continued, for a short while, to supervise the Board's last programme, assisted by an advisory council, until Law No. 74 of 1959 abolished the Ministry of Development and created an Economic Planning Board, a Ministry of Industry and a Ministry of Planning.

The new Planning Board was a committee of ministers under the

20   ROLE OF GOVERNMENT IN INDUSTRIALIZATION OF IRAQ

chairmanship of the Prime Minister with membership of Ministers of Finance, Planning and those ministers whose ministries dealt with development such as Ministers of Industry, Agriculture, and Communication.

A planning committee composed of ministers who are most concerned with development and headed by the Prime Minister is in a strong position to make decisions which the Cabinet will accept and to facilitate co-ordination of the most important sectors' programmes in a development plan. But such a planning board has two serious weaknesses. First, it cannot provide continuity in the development work where there is political instability and frequent Cabinet changes. When the Planning Board was created, some people thought that the era of political instability was over. An observer, for example, argued that the main cause of political instability was the isolation of the previous regime from the people; since the Revolutionary Regime, he thought, has ended this situation, organizations based on it must be changed.[21] The Revolutionary Regime, however, did not provide political stability; in fact instability increased, thus during the period 1958–65 there were three successful 'revolutions' and a larger, but unknown, number of unsuccessful attempts, civil disorder and 16 Cabinet changes.[22]

The second main shortcoming of a Board composed of all operational ministers is that 'it places undue stress on compromise . . . and is likely to have difficulties dealing with issues which are not questions with simple answers but complicated alternatives'.[23] This presumably, is why Law No. 44 of 1964 made the Planning Board again a mixed committee of ministers and executive members, under the presidency of the Prime Minister with membership of the Ministers of Finance, Planning, Economy and the Governor of the Central Bank, and other ministers who would be called when projects concerning their ministries were discussed by the Board. The number of executive members was four only, which means that they were a minority in the new Board while they were a majority in the old Development Board.

According to the 1964 Law the tasks of the Planning Board were: 'preparation of a general detailed economic plan and annual plans; determination of economic, fiscal, monetary and commercial policies with the approval of the Council of Ministers; determination of methods and agencies which implement projects of the plan; supervision of the preparation of annual ordinary budget; supervision and direction of economic activities of the private sectors within the general framework of the plan; and *approval of all matters in connection with the implementation of any project whose total cost is more than I.D. 250,000.*'[24]

ORGANIZATION AND ADMINISTRATION OF GOVERNMENT 21

The Minister of Planning was the technical secretary of the Board and entrusted with the formulation of plans as well as preparation of various related economic, statistical and engineering analyses. The Ministry was organized into departments dealing with the main sectors of the economy, namely, agriculture, industry, building and communication. In addition, there were economic, legal, administrative and statistical departments each headed by a Director General.

Thus the Government set up a central planning organization which constituted the policy-making organ responsible for the determination of targets and priorities, as well as for the formulation of detailed plans. Plan implementation, however, was the responsibility of ministries. This was one of the main differences between the old Development Board organization and the new Planning Board. An important potential strength of the new organization was that it made it easier for the Planning Board to concentrate on general planning and to leave the implementation of projects, with their enormous amount of administrative and technical work, to the operational ministries, provided that the Planning Board and the Ministry of Planning were ready to delegate these responsibilities to ministries, and that the ministries were prepared to accept them.

A serious weakness of the new organization was that, unlike the Development Board, plan implementation agencies came directly under the control of the Ministry of Finance, which meant that these ministries could not increase their capacity to implement plans without the approval of the Ministry of Finance. The objectives of finance agencies and of planning agencies are different: 'finance thinks in terms of economy, planning in terms of development'.[25] A lesson of experience is that 'Ministers of Finance in less developed countries often pay little attention to central planner's plans'.[26] But if the Ministry of Finance chooses to ignore the need for expansion in the capacity of implementing ministries it can create serious obstacles to development. The need for co-ordination between the capital budget and the ordinary budget was important under the Development Board Organization, it became vital under the new organization.

3. *The Ministry of Industry*

Law No. 74 of 1959 created a Ministry of Industry to undertake all activities concerned with the industrialization of Iraq and to supervise both public and private industrial affairs. The following departments, which previously dealt with industrial affairs, were transferred to the Ministry:

C

22 ROLE OF GOVERNMENT IN INDUSTRIALIZATION OF IRAQ

1. The General Administration Board of the Ministry of Development.
2. The Department of Legal Affairs and contracts from the Ministry of Development.
3. The Third Technical Section of the Ministry of Development which dealt with industry, mining and electricity.
4. The Industrial Bank from the Ministry of Development.
5. The Department of Industry from the Ministry of Economy which was dealing with industrial research, and promotion of private industry.
6. All state industrial plants including Baghdad Electricity, The Nuclear Energy Authority, the Mining section of the Department of Oil Affairs of the Ministry of Economy and Federation of Industry.[27]

The Ministry's organization and tasks were defined in September 1959 and the Ministry included the following departments:

1. Department of Diwan for General Administration.
2. Department of Industrial Planning.
3. Department of Industrial Design and Construction.
4. Department of Industrial Buildings.
5. Department of Promotion of Private Industries.
6. The Industrial Bank.
7. Centre For Promotion of Industrial Management.
8. Department of Standardization and Specification.
9. National Electricity Authority.
10. The Organization for Management of State Manufacturing Plants and
11. Federation of Industry.[28]

This study deals only with those aspects of industrialization which are covered by those activities under 2, 3, 4, 5 and 6; we shall discuss later, in detail, the activities of 5 and 6 and shall deal below with the activities of the other three Departments.

The Department of Industrial Planning was created to collect data concerning industrialization, classify and analyse it to prepare an industrial plan within the framework of the general economic plan. This Department was also entrusted with the task of following up the industrial plan. It was organized into the following sections: economic studies, planning, statistics, laboratory research and administration.

Thus the planning machinery for the industrial section consisted of the Department of Industry in the Ministry of Planning, which represented the central planning organ for industry, and the Department of Industrial Planning of the Ministry of Industry as the counterpart at the sectional level. According to the Ministry of Industry's laws and regulations, the latter Department was responsible for drafting the sectoral plan to be submitted to the Ministry of Planning for finalization and co-ordination with other sectoral plans of the economy.[29]

With the exception of oil refineries, implementation of the state's industrial projects was entrusted to the Departments of Industrial Design and Construction and the Department of Industrial Buildings in the Ministry of Industry. The task of the former Department was the preparation of specifications and the construction of Government industrial projects. It was organized into the following sections: electricity and electrical industries, mining and metallic industries, spinning and weaving industries, chemical industries and construction materials industry. Each one of these represented various industrial sub-sections. The Department included also a civil engineering and an administration section containing a special unit to deal with problems of transport delays, and the insuring and storing of industrial machinery.[30] The Department of Industrial Buildings was entrusted with the construction of buildings connected with the industrial projects of the Ministry, and contained three sections for design, implementation and administration.[31]

After the reorganization of the Government's development administration in 1959, the industrial planning and implementation agencies became so numerous that one can hardly think of any aspect of industrial development which lacked a specific department to deal with it.[32] Thus the sections connected with economic and technical research of the Department of Industrial Planning in the Ministry of Industry, were supposed to study the economy and put forward ideas for the establishment of new projects, the section for industrial planning and statistics of the same department were supposed to carry out feasibility studies of these ideas covering markets, raw materials, labour, power etc. and then present them to the Ministry of Planning, which in turn was supposed to call on its Industrial Department to study the project from economic and technical points of view. After initial approval by the Planning Board, the Department of Design and Construction in the Ministry of Industry was supposed to prepare the specifications and designs of the project and then, after the project received final approval from the Board, to proceed with actual construction of the project, assisted by the Department of Industrial Buildings. Meanwhile, the section for manpower and experts of the Department of Industrial

24 ROLE OF GOVERNMENT IN INDUSTRIALIZATION OF IRAQ

Planning were supposed to provide the necessary skilled labour and experts to run the project when completed.

This is how the system should have worked according to the rules and regulations of these departments. In practice, however, actual proposals of projects, feasibility studies, designs and specifications, training of labour and actual construction of industrial projects were not dealt with according to the system, even for the simplest project.[33] Thus, although the Department of Industrial Buildings was supposed to design and construct industrial buildings, its activities were, nevertheless, confined only to supervising and following Iraq's share in the civil engineering and construction of industrial projects covered by the Iraqi-Soviet agreement of 1959.[34] Even here, however, Iraq's commitments were contracted out to the private sector.[35] On the other hand the Department of Industrial Design and Construction was not directly involved in the actual preparation of designs, specifications or construction of any project. The Department was evolved from the old third Technical Section of the Ministry of Development and like the old section, the new Department was confined to supervising work undertaken by consultants and contractors and similar tasks, such as provision of liaison between consultants, contractors and the Government.

As for the Department of Industrial Planning in the Ministry of Industry, it was supposed to study the economy, propose new projects, prepare feasibility studies and formulate a sectoral plan. In practice it did little, if anything, of this sort. This Department was evolved from the old Department of Industry of the Ministry of Economy which concentrated primarily on technical research and laboratory work and was 'not equipped to analyse and record commercial and economic operations of industry';[36] in other words the staff of this department was not familiar with the techniques of project appraisal and sector programming. The Department of Industrial Planning also continued to concentrate on laboratory research and during the period 1959–65 at no time had it had more than four graduates in economics in its planning and economic research sections.

Between the time when the Department was established (or more precisely since it assumed its new name), in 1959, and 1965, three 'general plans' were prepared by the Planning Board, but the Department proved to be so inadequate in its planning activities that the Government, on the recommendation of the Planning Board and Ministry of Planning, enacted Law No. 27 of 1965 in order to establish programming units in all ministries. This meant that a separate agency was established inside the Ministry of Industry to assume the responsibilities of industrial planning. Moreover, al-

ORGANIZATION AND ADMINISTRATION OF GOVERNMENT   25

most all the projects included in the industrial plans were proposed and studied by outsiders,[37] and the Department did not prepare feasibility studies for any project; such studies were undertaken by foreign consultants.

Furthermore, when, by 1965 most projects proposed by consultants were either established, or under implementation, and new projects were required, the Planning Board found it necessary to authorize the Ministry of Industry to contract with a consulting firm to prepare an industrial survey similar to that undertaken by A. D. Little, Inc. for the old Development Board nearly ten years earlier.[38] Such studies basically look for new projects and prepare a pre-feasibility study for them. Thus, it seems safe to argue that the enlarged organization for planning and implementation of industrial projects after 1959, represented no real improvement on the much smaller and simpler Third Technical Section of the old system.

Nor did the reorganization of 1959 change fundamentally the procedure followed by the Development Board in planning and implementing industrial projects.[39] In fact one can substitute the Planning Board for the Development Board, and the Ministry of Industry's Department of Design and Construction for the Third Technical Section, and repeat exactly what was said about the Development Board above to get a clear picture of the procedural method of planning and implementation after 1959. An important difference is that the implementation procedure in the new organization involved more departments inside the Ministry of Industry, on the one hand, and involved two Ministries—Planning and Industry—instead of one in the old organization, on the other hand. Of course, implementation always requires time-consuming cross-references between the different departments involved. But the amount of time needed for communication tends to be greater the larger the number of departments involved inside each ministry, and communication tends to be slower between two ministries than communication inside one ministry. Assuming no other changes, the whole process of planning and implementation tends to be slower in the new organization.

When organizations grow and become more complex, it is essential to reduce the need for time-consuming communication and maintain only essential cross-references. This could have been done by delegation of responsibility from the Planning Board, for example, down to the departments of the Ministry of Industry, but would have required a fundamental change in the outlook of top policy makers towards planning.

The re-organization of 1959, however, was not accompanied by such a change in the approach of the Planning Board towards planning. The 'Government announced in April 1959, that it intended

26 ROLE OF GOVERNMENT IN INDUSTRIALIZATION OF IRAQ

to decentralize to a substantial degree all matters connected with economic development',[40] and in fact, one of the main principles on which the re-organization of 1959 was based was the idea of decentralization, in the sense of a separation between planning and the implementation of investment programmes. The Planning Board was created to become a major planning body with the Ministry of Planning as its technical secretariat to help it in drawing development programmes. Ministries were established and made responsible for detailed planning and implementation of projects. The behaviour of the Planning Board and the Ministry of Planning vis-à-vis other ministries remained similar to the behaviour of the Development Board and the Ministry of Development towards their Technical Sections. A report by the World Bank pointed out in late 1963 that 'the Economic Planning Board, though officially at ministerial level, is preoccupied with details of project approval, award of contracts, even selection of personnel. The result is that little attention is given to basic issues of development policy and strategy on the one hand, nor on the other hand to the task of improving the administration machinery and procedures throughout the Government to make implementation more expeditious'.[41]

To indicate what preoccupation with the details of implementation involves I need only quote the Five-Year Plan 1961–65, which made the Planning Board responsible for 'assignment of consulting engineers, approval of economic and technical reports and the preliminary specification of projects, approval of general conditions of tenders and contracts, approval of technical specifications, and final designs of projects, the method according to which a project must be implemented, announcement of tenders and extension of terms, awarding of tenders, and changes in specifications, approval of necessary appropriations for projects dealing with compensations, delays, arbitrations etc., disposal of movable and immovable property of the project, approval of completion of the project, approval of budgets, statements and programmes prepared for spending on projects, appointment of foreign engineers and employees for the purpose of implementation of the plan, changing of sites of projects, suspension of work on a project or part of it, transfer of necessary funds for the continuation of a project from the annual appropriation of subsequent years to the preceding year for which the allocations are exhausted, and the insertion of the names of contractors dealing with the Board in the blacklist should it be required by public interest'.[42]

Now the bulk of these functions are purely administrative. Thus, beside preparation of the detailed plans the Board monitored in

ORGANIZATION AND ADMINISTRATION OF GOVERNMENT 27

minute details the implementation of projects and in this sense planning was highly centralized. Such a system may be tolerable when the plan includes few projects, and the administrative machinery is efficient, and members of the Board can therefore devote a fairly large amount of their time to plans. But neither of these conditions was satisfied in Iraq. Plans included a large number of projects: for example, the 1961–65 plan included nearly 300 projects of which 30 were industrial; it involved expenditure of more than I.D. 560 million (which was almost equal to the total government ordinary budget during the same period). Most of the projects were large, involving several consultants and contractors for each project, while the implementation process took several years.

It is clear that concentration of decision-making for the administrative and technical details of such a large number of projects 'poses insuperable problems for communication. Few individuals at the apex of the pyramid find themselves challenged to make quickly a range of decisions which would require supernatural capabilities'.[43] Moreover, in Iraq, these few individuals were not in a position to devote their whole time to planning. The Board until 1964 was a committee of ministers and throughout 1959–65 it included the Prime Minister and the Minister of Finance, who clearly had other important responsibilities. Under these circumstances, no matter how efficient is the implementing machinery, the whole process will be slowed down by the bottlenecks of top-level review. On the other hand, the time consuming tasks of reviewing project selection, evaluation, preparation and implementation prevented the Board, according to an I.B.R.D. study, from undertaking its more vital tasks of general planning, such as the assessment of total resources, selection of alternative patterns of investment and the formulation of policy.[44]

4. Administrative Defects

An efficient bureaucracy may reduce delays caused by concentration of decision-making in the centre, but one can hardly expect to find an effective and efficient bureaucracy in almost all developing countries. The efficiency of the bureaucracy depends on the ability of the people employed by the Government. Personnel requirements can be divided into three categories, namely, administrative, technical and clerical. In Iraq the first two were understandably short in both number and qualifications and the third in qualifications.[45]

The World Bank Mission noticed in 1950 that the number of students in technical schools was inadequate for the needs of Iraq.[46] As to quality, the same mission reported that, for example, the

28 ROLE OF GOVERNMENT IN INDUSTRIALIZATION OF IRAQ

College of Commerce and Economics 'apparently produces neither competent and practical book-keepers and accountants, nor people well grounded in economics and finance capable of acting as company secretaries or as economic and financial experts in business or Government'.[47] In fact, the shortage in the number of qualified people was so acute that, according to a member of the Development Board, it would have been a miracle if the bureaucracy had been able to expand to cope with the increased amount of work implicit in Iraq's development programmes.[48]

Certain personnel practices also imposed serious strains on efficiency in Iraq's public administration. The inadequacy of pay scales lowered morale, discouraged efficiency, and forced employees to look for other sources of income, including dishonesty. 'Many civil servants were compelled to supplement their salaries by engaging in business, or accepting other employment with resulting neglect of their official duties'.[49] Rank and pay in Iraq depend largely upon scholastic attainment which according to Lord Salter, 'bears little relation to merit or aptitude. At one end of the scale young persons who may not be fit for any other employment are able to enter the civil service at a fixed salary because they have spent the requisite number of years in a primary, intermediate or secondary school. On the other hand, students who have spent many years studying abroad and have gained high educational qualities are discouraged from entering the Service because they will receive the same low salary as a person who, for example, has passed four years in the Law College'.[50]

The World Bank Mission noticed that promotion was based 'almost entirely on seniority and other considerations rather than on merit'.[51] No doubt that seniority, in the sense of maturity and cumulative experience, is a relevant consideration in promotion, but in Iraq seniority meant merely time spent in the service. Moreover, frequent cabinet changes encouraged bureaucrats to become involved in partisan politics; they 'took sides with prospective ministers. When these ministers achieved power, their friends were amply rewarded. Such a spoils system, needless to say, had a very damaging effect on the efficiency and morale of Government administration.'[52] This discouraged civil servants from concentrating on their work and improving their efficiency because under such a system they feel that their advancement depends on chances of political or personal favouritism rather than on their ability.

Another wasteful practice was the misplacing of people. Thus, as Adams put it, 'it takes luck, influence or both for a person to be assigned where he can make the best use of specialized training'.[53] Moreover, 'officials were frequently shifted from one position to

ORGANIZATION AND ADMINISTRATION OF GOVERNMENT 29

another without regard to their qualities and experience'.[54] This was partly caused by political instability, and after each Cabinet change a number of senior civil servants were removed. For example, in 1963, a World Bank Mission reported that it had 'heard unofficial estimates that one-half to three-quarters of the people in Government posts involving any real degree of responsibility were new in their jobs since the February coup'.[55] This, admittedly, is an extreme example but all observers have stressed the unfavourable consequences of frequent shifts of senior civil servants on efficiency. Under such a system it is difficult for the Civil Service to provide continuity of administrative experience for the benefit of successive Governments. Moreover, it means that officers do not stay in one department long enough to become really useful.

Serious defects are also to be found in paper work, registry and archives. Details of this kind may seem to be unimportant, but 'proper filing and storage of paper can be a practical contribution to sound administration, and in more than one country it has been suggested as a very appropriate starting point for reform'.[56] Although I have not come across any document on this aspect of Iraq's civil administration, three years of work inside the Ministry of Industry has convinced me that reform might as well start from here. The filing system of the Ministry, for example, was such that incoming papers, reports, memoranda, and minutes were stored in a manner that made subsequent retrieval, sometimes impossible. The time required to recover a document (if possible at all) was sometimes more than a week.

All these and other defects seriously affected the efficiency of public administration. Although the weakness of Government machinery was officially recognized, it seems that not enough continuous attention was paid to the improvement of the administration before 1958 and by that time, according to one authority, 'the administration was cracking seriously'.[57] After the Revolution of 1958 little systematic attention was paid to this vital question and the quality of the administration remained 'the most crucial element in Iraq's development effort'.[58]

REFERENCES

1. Hanson, A. H., *The Process of Planning, A Study of India's Five-Year Plans*, p. 268
2. I.B.R.D., *Economic Development of Iraq*, p. 77
3. *Ibid.*, pp. 77–8
4. *Ibid.*, p. 56
5. U.N., *A Handbook of Public Administration, Current Concepts and Practice, with Special Reference to Developing Countries*, p. vii
6. Qubain, *Reconstruction of Iraq*, p. 32; al-Jalili, *Lectures on Economics of Iraq*, p. 193 and al-Jamali, *Iraq Past and Present*, p. 26

30 ROLE OF GOVERNMENT IN INDUSTRIALIZATION OF IRAQ

7. Government of Iraq, Law No. 23, 1950
8. Government of Iraq, Law No. 24, 1952
9. Qubain, *op. cit.*, p. 35 and Adams, *Iraq's People and Resources*, p. 104
10. The Development Board and the Ministry of Development, *Second Development Week*, p. 10
11. Lord Salter, *The Development of Iraq: A Plan of Action*, p. 97
12. al-Jalili, *Lectures on Economics of Iraq*, p. 192
13. Adams, *Iraq's People and Resources*, p. 104
14. Salter, *The Development of Iraq*, pp. 97–98
15. Khadduri, *Independent Iraq*, p. 372
16. *Ibid.*, p. 358
17. Langley, *Industrialization of Iraq*, p. 205
18. *Ibid.*, p. 205
19. *Ibid.*, pp. 206–7
20. Salter, *Economic Development of Iraq*, p. 103
21. Hassan, *Studies in Economics of Iraq*, p. 229
22. Information collected by Dr. A. Kelidar from several issues of *The Middle East Journal* (The Middle East Institute, Washington, D.C.) and *Chronology of Arab Politics* (American University of Beirut).
23. Waterson, *Development Planning*, p. 490
24. Government of Iraq, Law No. 44, 1964
25. Hanson, *The Process of Planning*, p. 79
26. Waterson, *Development Planning*, p. 391
27. Government of Iraq, Law No. 74, 1959
28 Ministry of Industry, *Compilation of Law and Regulations concerning Industry*, pp. 6, 11, 59
29. *Ibid.*, p. 7
30. *Ibid.*, p. 8
31. *Ibid.*, p. 11
32. An important section missing from the new organization was a unit to deal with improvement in the administration itself. This is not to be confused with the administration sections in each department, which dealt with the 'household' business of that department. In fact, improvement in organization seems to be nobody's major duty or regular responsibility.
33. U.N., *Industrial Planning, Programming and Policies in Selected Countries of the Middle East*, pp. 57–58
34. For some details of this agreement see Chapter III—the Fourth Plan.
35. U.N., *Industrial Planning in Selected Countries of the Middle East*, p. 57
36. I.B.R.D., *Economic Development of Iraq*, p. 298
37. This point is discussed in Chapter III
38. Government of Iraq, Law No. 78, 1965 of Five-Year Plan 1965–69, p. 23 and Arthur D. Little, *A Plan for Industrial Development in Iraq.*
39. Jalal, F., *The Implementation Time Path of the Rayon Project in Iraq; A Case Study*, p. 1
40. Langley, *Industrialization of Iraq*, pp. 307–8
41. I.B.R.D. International Development Association, *Current Economic Position and Prospects of Iraq*, September 1963, p. 7
42. Government of Iraq, Law No. 70, 1961 of Five-Year Detailed Plan 1961–65, paragraph 7 of article 7
43. Riggs, *Administration in Developing Countries, The Theory of Prismatic Society*, p. 283
44. I.B.R.D., *Current Economic Position and Prospects of Iraq*, p. 7
45. al-Jalili, *Lectures on Economics of Iraq*, p. 257
46. I.B.R.D., *Economic Development of Iraq*, p. 257

ORGANIZATION AND ADMINISTRATION OF GOVERNMENT 31

47. *Ibid.*, p. 297
48. Ionides, *Divide and Lose*, p. 125
49. I.B.R.D., *Economic Development of Iraq*, p. 78
50. Salter, *The Development of Iraq*, p. 238
51. I.B.R.D., *op. cit.*, p. 78
52. Khadduri, *Independent Iraq*, p. 60
53. Adams, *op. cit.*, p. 131
54. I.B.R.D., *Economic Development of Iraq*, p. 78
55. I.B.R.D., *Current Economic Position and Prospects of Iraq*, p. 7
56. U.N., *A Handbook of Public Administration*, p. 28
57. Ionides, *Divide and Lose*, pp. 201–2
58. I.B.R.D., *Current Economic Position and Prospects of Iraq*, p. 6

Chapter III

FORMULATION OF GOVERNMENT INVESTMENT PROGRAMMES: 1951–65

The aim of this chapter is to analyse programmes formulated by both the Planning Board and the Development Board for the investment of oil revenues in different sectors of the economy. The formulation of economic plans is discussed from the point of view of the size of investment programmes and the allocation of investment resources among different sectors and projects, in order to discover whether or not there was any improvement over the period in planning techniques. Special emphasis is put on the industrial investment programmes which were adopted as part of the general investment plans. The word 'plans' is used instead of the more accurate phrase 'government investment programmes' for the sake of brevity.

1. *Plans of the Development Board, 1951–58*

In the early 1950s the Government entrusted the Development Board with the task of investing 70% of oil revenues in order to raise the standard of living of the people of Iraq. The Board began to operate towards the end of 1950, and until it was abolished in 1958, it formulated three investment programmes which are summarized in Table III.1. We will call them the first, the second and third plans.

The First Plan, 1951–56: This plan called for the expenditure of I.D. 155.4 million or I.D. 25.7 million per annum, compared to I.D. 11.5 million under the last capital budget 1949–53, formulated by the Government, following the traditional extraordinary budget procedure.[1] Compared with the previous capital budgets this was a very ambitious plan indeed and was bound to have far reaching economic effects. It was also much more diversified than any previous extraordinary budget in that it contained a larger number of projects and included industry, which had not been included in the earlier capital budgets. The vote for industry, mining and electricity of I.D. 31 million in the plan represented 20% of the total plan investment.

No allocation was made, however, for specific industrial pro-

FORMULATION OF GOVT. INVESTMENT PROGRAMMES

TABLE III.1

Plans of the Development Board

| | I.D. Million | | | | | |
| | The First Plan 1951–56 | | The Second Plan 1955–59 | | The Third Plan 1955–60 | |
	I.D.	%	I.D.	%	I.D.	%
Agriculture	66·1	42·5	114·4	37·6	168·1	33·6
Industry	31·1	20·0	43·6	14·3	67·1	13·4
Transport	29·0	18·7	74·2	24·4	124·4	24·9
Buildings	20·6	13·3	60·7	20·0	123·1	24·6
Miscellaneous	8·6	5·5	11·4	3·7	17·3	3·5
Total	155·4	100·0	304·3	100·0	500·0	100·0

Source: The Development Board, *Compilation of Laws concerning the Development Board*, pp. 8–9; The Development Board and the Ministry of Development, Law No. 43 of 1955 for the General Programme of the Development Board and the Ministry of Development, pp. 16–23; Development Board and the Ministry of Development, Law No. 54 of 1956 for the Amendment of Law No. 43, 1955, p. 11

jects due to lack of preliminary studies on the basis of which costs could be estimated. The World Bank Mission's report included a preliminary survey of Iraq's industrial resources and suggested several industries with development potential. In addition the Industrial Bank of Iraq had already employed consultants to examine industrial projects.[2] On the basis of these studies the Board decided to build a number of industrial projects, to undertake mineral and industrial surveys and to increase the country's capacity to supply electricity.[3] By the end of the first plan the Bitumen Refinery of Quiyara was under construction to produce 60,000 tons of bitumen annually, the Cotton Spinning and Weaving Mill of Mosul was under construction to produce one million square yards of cotton textiles, two cement plants at Sulaimaniya and Mosul were under construction each to produce 350 tons of cement per day, with financial aid from the Board, the Government Oil Refinery Administration completed a refinery at Doura with a total capacity of one million tons per year.[4]

The World Bank Mission suggested, and the Board agreed, that a chemical plant, should be constructed at the oil fields at Kirkuk to utilize the natural gas. Moreover, the Mission considered that natural gas produced as a by-product of oil and almost totally wasted was a most promising industrial asset for Iraq. It proposed a plant of a capacity capable of producing annually 500,000 tons of ammonium sulphate, 100,000 tons of elemental sulphur, and 300,000 tons of cement.[5] In 1953 the Board hired consultants to

34 ROLE OF GOVERNMENT IN INDUSTRIALIZATION OF IRAQ

prepare a feasibility study. They found that a plant on the scale envisaged could be erected at a total cost of I.D. 32.7 million which, on the basis of the prices ruling at that time, could make 15% profit on capital after allowing for amortization of the plant over a period of 20 years. The Board felt that this sum was very large and that the project would produce much more than the local market could absorb. It hesitated to commit funds on such a scale and asked the consultants to prepare a feasibility study for a smaller project. The consultants then prepared a study for a project to produce annually 250,000 tons of ammonium sulphate, 50,000 tons of elemental sulphur and 100,000 tons of cement at a total cost of I.D. 20.7 million, which could earn 9.3% profit on capital. The same consultants also submitted supplementary reports on a large number of chemical products which could be produced from gas. But the Board decided to wait for another consultant's report.[6]

A survey of the country's mineral resources was important to reveal the industrial potentialities of Iraq, and the Board decided to finance a geological survey of the country. It hired a firm to carry out this survey in two stages: First, to locate areas containing minerals and to estimate their potential value, and second to make experimental borings to ascertain whether exploitation would be worthwhile. Actual work on the first stage began early in 1954, and preliminary reports indicated the existence of large quantities of glass sand, limestone suitable for cement, bitumen and sulphur deposits.[7]

In 1954 the consultant firm which was hired by the Board to prepare an electric power survey, presented a report which established the foundation for Iraq's power programme. The report covers all power resources of the country, which, in addition to oil and natural gas, include the possibility of hydroelectric generation from dams and barrages. The report estimated the potential load for the next 20 years, proposed alternative methods of generation and suggested a programme for the development of power plants and transmission lines. It found that the immediate development of hydroelectric facilities was not economically sound. It suggested the immediate implementation of the first stage of the programme, which was the establishment of large power plants in the north, middle and south of the country. By the end of the plan the northern project was in the stage of preparing final specifications while the other two were still under review.[8]

During the first plan period the Board found itself considering many industrial proposals as a result of which it decided to undertake a general industrial survey to analyse potential industries that might be built and provide information on their priority.[9]

FORMULATION OF GOVT. INVESTMENT PROGRAMMES 35

The Second Plan, 1955–59: In April 1955 the Minister of Development presented to the Parliament a five-year plan to supersede the first plan. The new plan was necessary because of a sharp increase in oil revenues far exceeding original estimates, of changing conditions that made the cost estimates of the first plan no longer realistic, and of changes which were introduced in the 1953 Law with respect to the financing by the Board of projects of other departments.[10]

The plan proposed a total expenditure of I.D. 304.3 million, which was almost double that of the previous plan. The main difference, however, between this plan and the first one, aside from the size, was that the new plan included the so-called minor projects which were to be financed by the Board but implemented by other Government departments. Total allocation of funds for minor projects was I.D. 38.2 million or 10% of the total, out of which I.D. 32.3 million went to minor public buildings.

This plan allocated for industry, mining and power I.D. 43.6 million which represents 14.3% of total allocation. The plan was drawn after four years of experience during which an organization to deal with industry was set up (the Third Technical Section), and several important studies were carried out. The result was an industrial programme which was not only bigger than the previous one but different in form; while specific projects were not included in the first plan, the second plan subdivided the industrial sector as in Table III.2.

TABLE III.2

The Industrial Sector of the Second Plan, 1955–59

	I.D. 000
Bitumen Refinery Plant	855
Cotton Textile Plant	3,115
Mosul Cement Plant	2,208
Sulaimaniya Cement Plant	2,150
Mosul Sugar Plant	1,782
Electricity Projects	10,000
Mineral Survey	543
Industrial Survey	17
Laboratory Tools	900
Other Industries	22,000
Total	43,570

Source: Development Board and Ministry of Development, Law No. 43, 1955, p. 21

In an explanatory note to the plan it was mentioned that the I.D. 22 million devoted to the item 'other industries' would be invested in profitable industrial projects recommended by the consultants

36 ROLE OF GOVERNMENT IN INDUSTRIALIZATION OF IRAQ

then studying this sector, and that if they recommended the implementation of projects that required more funds, the Board would raise its allocation for this sector.[11]

This plan was operative for one year only (1955–56) but during this period the consultants, Arthur D. Little, Inc., who were commissioned by the Board to undertake an industrial survey, presented their report. This report suggested a programme to be implemented in six years and contemplated the creation of a chemical industry, establishment of a steel rolling mill, a steel furnace, date industries, as well as expansion and improvement of the existing industries at a total cost of I.D. 43 million. It suggested also a group of other industries for further investigation, such as pharmaceutical products and glassware. It also referred to a number of industries and argued that they were not suitable for Iraq for some time to come for various reasons, including agricultural machinery, and fruit and vegetable canning.[12]

The chemical industry was the central focus of the Little report. But the report made it clear that the chemical industry was complex and that costs of production were closely related to plant size. Moreover, one plant often produces a number of joint products or by-products and unless markets can be found for the extra products, it may not be profitable to produce the main product. It stated that 'investigation has disclosed that the establishment in Iraq of plants to produce rayon and paper and to recover sulphur from natural gas is economically justified. A rayon plant and a paper mill of the recommended size would between them require 5,600 tons annually of caustic soda. This, coupled with the demand of existing industries, would, by 1960, result in a probable total demand of 8,000 tons of caustic soda, which would justify its production in Iraq. The only method of producing this chemical that would be economical on this scale, the electric method, would result in the production of about 0.9 ton of chlorine for each ton of caustic soda produced. Unless markets can be found for this, it would be cheaper to import the caustic soda. The proposed plastic material industry offers a potential market for chlorine, as it is required as a raw material for polyvinyl chloride. Natural gas can be used to produce ethylene, a raw material for both polyvinyl chloride and polyethylene, which are widely used plastics with a growing world market.

'The sulphur in the Kirkuk natural gas could supply, in addition to export markets, the rayon plant with the sulphur and sulphuric acid it would need. At the same time, it would make it possible to produce fertilizers in Iraq, as sulphur would be required in substantial quantities to produce ammonium sulphate. Ammonium sulphate

FORMULATION OF GOVT. INVESTMENT PROGRAMMES 37

or other nitrogenous fertilizers, ammonium nitrate and urea, would require ammonia, which could also be manufactured from natural gas.'[13]

The Little report, therefore, made clear the complementarity between a complex of plants in the chemical industry; hence the need for an integrated properly phased and well balanced industrial programme.

The Third Plan, 1955–60: The main reasons put forward for presenting this plan in May 1956 to replace the 1955–59 plan were the increased oil revenues, the completion of several studies, especially in the fields of drainage, communications and housing, and recommendations of Lord Salter in favour of the more flexible and more diversified programme.[14]

The plan called for the expenditure of I.D. 500 million including I.D. 49 million which was in the 1955 allocation under the previous plan; this left an annual expenditure of I.D. 90.8 million in the following five years. The plan increased greatly the allocation of funds for projects geared to meet immediate human needs such as hospitals, clinics, drinking water etc. It was also made more flexible, contemplating new projects which might or might not be implemented depending on whether they were found economically sound after careful study. The Minister of Development could also propose, on behalf of the Board, supplementary programmes in the light of new studies or if oil revenues changed sharply.

The plan devoted I.D. 67.1 million to industry which was 13% more than the allocation for industry in the second plan, but the share of industry in total funds of the plan decreased to 13.4% compared to 14.3% in the previous plan. Most of the absolute increase devoted to industry went to the item 'other industries'. Table III.3 shows that other items were similar to the previous plan and

TABLE III.3

The Industrial Sector of the Third Plan, 1955–60

	I.D. 000
Bitumen Refinery Plant	67
Cotton Textile Plant	3,623
Mosul Cement Plant	3,243
Sulaimaniya Cement Plant	2,455
Mosul Sugar Plant	2,917
Mineral Survey	126
Electricity Projects	12,669
Other Industries	37,900
1955 Allocation for all Items	4,119
Total	67,119

Source: The Development Board and the Ministry of Development, Law No. 54, 1956, p. 25

38 ROLE OF GOVERNMENT IN INDUSTRIALIZATION OF IRAQ

changes reflected actual expenditure during the previous year (1955), and some refinements in cost estimates. Total expenditure for the five manufacturing industrial projects were given and subdivided into different elements, i.e. machinery, building, power etc., each industrial project included a housing project which accounts for more than 20% of the total cost in some cases.[15]

The projects under the item 'other industries' were basically embodiments of several industries proposed by the Little report, as shown in Table III.4.

TABLE III.4

Projects Suggested by the Little Report and Included in the Third Plan

	I.D. 000
Extension and Improvement of Existing Industries	11,500
New Industrial Projects:	
Sulphur Extraction, Paper, Date Syrup, Animal Fodder, Steel Rolling Mill, Steel Furnace, Rayon and Rayon Textile	12,300
Industries for which studies must be completed:	
Fertilizer, Plastic Materials, Caustic Soda, Natural Gas Pipeline	10,700
Other Industries	4,670
Total	39,170

Source: The Development Board and Ministry of Development, Law No. 54, 1956, p. 31

2. *Programmes of the Planning Board, 1959–65*

The Planning Board was established in 1959, and up to 1965 it had formulated three industrial programmes which are summarized in Table III.5. These programmes will be be called the Fourth, the Fifth and the Sixth Plans.

The Fourth Plan, 1959–62: The aim of this plan was to 'change radically the direction of the plan of the previous regime . . . in a

TABLE III.5

Investment Programmes of the Planning Board 1959–65,
I.D. Million

	The Fourth Plan 1959–62		The Fifth Plan 1961–65		The Sixth Plan 1965–69	
	I.D.	%	I.D.	%	I.D.	%
Agriculture	47·9	12·2	112·9	20·3	173	25·9
Industry	38·7	9·8	166·8	29·9	187	28·1
Transport	100·8	25·7	136·4	24·5	110	16·5
Buildings	191·5	48·7	140·1	25·2	134	20·1
Miscellaneous	14·0	3·6	0·0	0·0	62	9·3
Total	392·9	100·0	556·2	100·0	666·0	100·0

Source: Ministry of Guidance Law No. 181, 1959, p. 11; The Five Years Detailed Economic Plan, 1961–65, issued by the Ministry of Guidance, Baghdad, 1962, pp. 11, 79 and Ministry of Guidance Law No. 87 (1965) of the Five Years Economic Plan 1965–69, p. 71

manner which can serve the interests of Iraqi people', because the new Government believed that 'oil revenues have been wasted on matters of no interest to Iraq'.[16] Thus the Revolutionary Government reduced the share of oil revenues going to capital formation from 70% to 50% and formulated a plan which gave first priority to public buildings and housing, to which it devoted I.D. 191.5 million representing 48.7% of total allocation.

The plan allocated I.D. 38.7 million to the industrial sector, which represented 9.8% of total allocations. This, however, did not include the amount of funds required for the projects of the Iraqi-Soviet agreement of 1959, which included a steel mill, a fertilizer plant, a sulphur extraction plant, a woollen textile plant, a cotton textile mill, a clothing workshop, a plant to produce agricultural machinery, a stocking and underwear factory, an electric bulb factory, a canning factory, a glassware factory, a pharmaceutical factory and a plant for the production of electrical equipment. The agreement also provided for technical assistance in the establishments of plants to produce caustic soda, polyvinyl chloride and polyethylene. Studies and designs of these projects were to be carried out during 1959–60 while most machinery and equipment was to be delivered during 1961–62. The capacity of each factory was mentioned in the agreement and Iraq was made responsible for civil engineering and provision of all available Iraqi materials and labour. In cases where this was not adequate, the Soviets were to provide them.[17] But the amount of funds required for these projects were not mentioned in the plan, because at that time even rough estimates of their costs were not available. The plan, however, devoted I.D. 10 million to cover Iraq's share in the cost of all projects covered by the agreement, which numbered 61, but this sum was not divided between different sectors. Almost all the industrial projects of the agreement were derived from previous preliminary studies and plans. In fact, with the exception of the electrical bulb factory and the electrical equipment plant, all these projects were mentioned in the Development Board Plans and the Little report.[18]

Beside the projects of the agreement Table III.6 shows that the plan included all other projects of the Development Board, it also included a shoe factory, and a cigarette manufacturing project which was previously carried out by the Government-operated Tobacco Monopoly.[19]

The Fifth Plan, 1961–65: This plan gave the highest priority to the industrial sector to which it devoted I.D. 166.7 million representing almost 30% of total allocation. This sum was divided into I.D. 161 million for major industrial projects and I.D. 5.7 million for

40 ROLE OF GOVERNMENT IN INDUSTRIALIZATION OF IRAQ

TABLE III.6

The Industrial Sector of the Fourth Plan 1959–62

	I.D. 000
Mosul Sugar Plant	260
Sulaimaniya Sugar Plant	4,000
Date Syrup Plant	300
Natural Gas Pipeline	1,100
Mosul Cement Plant	192
Sulaimaniya Cigarette Factory	1,000
Rayon and Rayon Textile Plants	100
Paper Plant	10,000
Popular Shoes Plant	350
Electricity	21,384
Projects of the Agreement	—
Total	38,636

Source: Ministry of Guidance, Law No. 181, 1959, pp. 33–5

the so-called complementary projects of which I.D. 4.3 million was devoted to minor electricity projects of the Ministry of Municipalities. The major industrial projects are summarized in table III.7. The plan provided funds for each project for different years and in the case of the projects of the Iraqi-Soviet agreement, the total allocation was divided between the two parties.

The chemical industry of the plan included caustic soda, ethylene, polyethylene, polyvinyl chloride, carbon black, rayon yarn,

TABLE III.7

The Industrial Sector of the Fifth Plan, 1961–65

	No. of Projects	*I.D. 000*
Chemical Industries	10	36,450
Medical Projects	1	3,800
Cigarette Factory	1	1,650
Foodstuff Projects	3	4,810
Glass and Ceramic Plants	2	6,000
Electrical Products Plants	2	4,850
Metal Industries	3	17,564
Textile and Clothing Projects	6	23,733
Basrah Oil Refinery	1	10,000
Mineral Survey and Pipelines	4	8,850
Electricity	12	38,070
Atomic Energy Projects	3	2,700
Vocational Training Projects	1	1,850
Total		160,327

Source: Ministry of Guidance, Law No. 70, 1961, pp. 83–96

FORMULATION OF GOVT. INVESTMENT PROGRAMMES   41

paper, sulphur extraction, fertilizer, rubber tyres and tube factories. The metal industries included steel, agricultural machinery and geological equipment repair plants. The weaving and clothing industry included the clothing workshops, the stocking and underwear plant, the shoe factory, and the cotton, rayon and woollen textile plants. These were all the projects of the previous plan.

The Sixth Plan, 1965–69: This plan, like the previous one, gave first priority to industry but it raised the share of agriculture in total funds from fourth to second place. The new plan did not distinguish between major and minor or complementary projects. The latter projects were not complementary to the major projects as one might expect, but to minor projects which were previously financed by the ordinary budget.[20] But the plan included almost all the minor projects of the previous plan.

Table III.8 below summarizes the industrial sector of the sixth plan. The first item included all the projects of the previous plan

TABLE III.8

The Industrial Sector of the Sixth Plan, 1965–69

	No. of Projects	I.D. 000
1. Chemical Industries	10	47,450
2. Medical Projects	1	3,300
3. Foodstuff Projects	4	5,500
4. Glass and Ceramic Plants	2	4,500
5. Electrical Products Plants	2	1,500
6. Metal Industries	3	13,070
7. Textile and Clothing Projects	5	21,100
8. Oil Refining and Gas Pipeline	3	26,150
9. Mineral Survey	1	800
10. Electricity	10	39,550
11. Atomic Energy Projects	3	1,550
12. Vocational Training	3	2,530
13. Miscellaneous Projects		10,050
Total		177,050

Source: Ministry of Guidance, Law No. 87, 1965, pp. 15–23

except the carbon black project whose place was taken by a project for the production of rayon pulp. The second, fourth, fifth, sixth, ninth, and eleventh items included exactly the same projects as the previous plan. Items three, seven, and eight included all the projects of the previous plan plus the extension of Mosul textile and sugar plants and an oil refinery at Mosul. All these are negligible differences.

The novelty in the new plan was the provision (in item 13) of I.D. 4.6 million for 'new industrial projects', which included trac-

42 ROLE OF GOVERNMENT IN INDUSTRIALIZATION OF IRAQ

tor and motor car assembly, a project for production of salt, a chipboard project, laboratories for a specifications and standardization department, a woollen textile project in the north and an industrial survey of the Arthur D. Little type. The plan also devoted I.D. 5 million to cover working capital requirements of projects expected to be completed during the plan period. All these are summarized in item 13 of Table III.8. Nevertheless, it is hard to say that there was any significant difference between the projects included in this plan and in the previous one.

It is clear now that the process of implementation of the industrial programmes was extremely slow. Thus most of the projects included in the last plan of the Development Board were included in the 1965–69 plan; among these projects were the sulphur extraction, paper, steel, rayon yarn, rayon textile, fertilizer, plastic materials, caustic soda, gas pipeline etc. A large number of these were still under consideration in 1965 after they had been included in all these plans for more than 10 years. I will deal with this problem in detail in the next chapter.

3. Size of the Plans, 1951–65

Before 1950 Iraq was a poor country with a low investment ratio and a slow rate of economic progress. Any attempt to increase the saving ratio could have resulted in lowering the already low level of consumption. After 1950 a large increase in the investment ratio became possible without any need to restrain consumption. This was due to a substantial increase in oil revenues which could be used for immediate consumption, for investment purposes or for both in varying combinations.

Because the standard of living of the mass of the population was very low, one might argue that a large share of available oil revenues should have been devoted to current consumption. One may go further and support this view by arguing that an immediate betterment in the standard of living by improvements in health, education, food and housing conditions would increase productivity. In addition, so far as past savings habits of the population reflected the society's time preference, the case for devoting a large part of oil revenues to consumption purposes is strengthened.

On the other hand one can argue that Iraq had developed a level of consumption compatible with its productivity, it was, therefore, socially acceptable and politically feasible to maintain this level for the time being or to increase it slowly and push the rate of investment to a much higher level. Furthermore, as oil is an exhaustible asset and the revenues from it are subject to short-run instability from political disturbances, or from a sharp decline in oil prices

FORMULATION OF GOVT. INVESTMENT PROGRAMMES 43

due to a possible surplus of supply, it seemed proper to exploit the opportunity and push the investment of oil revenues to the highest possible level.

In 1950 the Government decided to use all oil revenues for investment purposes as we have seen, and the whole of the revenue was devoted to the Development Board to be used for capital formation.[21] Two years later the share of the Board was reduced to 70% and the remainder went to the government's ordinary budget to enable other public departments to carry out minor capital works independently of the Board. Changes came with Law No. 27, 1953 which made a distinction between major development projects and minor capital works. The Board became responsible for the finance and implementation of the first category of projects, while other Government departments assumed responsibility for the execution of the second category of projects, but they obtained finance from the Board's budget. This implied that the 30% of oil revenues falling to the Government could be used for current expenditure. This step made possible a substantial increase in Government services such as health and education, as well as the abolition of some indirect taxes levied upon basic food necessities in order to permit an increase in current consumption. In other words, the Government decided to use the revenues partly to increase the standard of living immediately, but mainly for capital formation designed to raise the standard of living in the future.

Since the increase in oil revenue was very large and the absorptive capacity of the economy was very limited at the beginning, this arrangement for using oil revenues appeared to be wise and the economy moved in the right direction, as will be demonstrated in Chapter IV.

The optimum investment ratio[22] might, however, be lower or higher than the level which available oil revenues could support at any time. Thus, to establish a direct relationship between oil revenues and the investment programme was not necessarily wise; in this respect the Planning Board's approach of deciding a target rate of growth of output, which under certain assumptions determined the rate of investment, seems superior to the Development Board's approach of investing a certain percentage of oil revenues. The first approach implied a commitment to a certain volume of investment and high-lighted the requirements for growth. Thus a political authority who wanted the economy to grow at a specific rate would have to find the necessary funds to finance it, while the second approach did not commit the Government to a difficult problem; if there were oil revenues, the investment ratio might be high, but if there were not enough oil revenues, failure to invest

44 ROLE OF GOVERNMENT IN INDUSTRIALIZATION OF IRAQ

the amounts required by the plans could conveniently be explained by the external factor, oil.

For Iraq, however, what matters most is not the approach to planning but the political commitment to feasible projects and determined action towards their implementation. The rate of growth selected by the Planning Board—to double national income in 10 years, representing an 8% growth rate in national income per year,[23] is not an exceptionally ambitious target, but it required a rate of public investment which could not be financed by only 50% of available oil revenues. Such a rate of growth needed over 70% of the revenues.[24] When in 1959 the Government reduced to 50% the share of oil revenues allocated to development, it became clear that it was not prepared to support such a high rate of growth. The planners' list of finances other than oil revenues cannot be taken as serious acts of economic calculation.[25] To increase, or even to maintain, the pre-1958 investment ratio, the share of oil revenues devoted to the capital budgets, would have had to be increased, not reduced in favour of public consumption accompanied by futile attempts to find other sources of finance for the plan. When the share of oil revenues allocated to ordinary budget is increased, the Ministry of Planning is in no position to find other sources of finance to raise the investment ratio to the level necessary to obtain the desired rate of growth of income.[26] When the development plan's share was reduced to 50% of oil revenues in 1959, the investment ratio and the amount of public capital expenditure were put under further pressure.[27]

4. *The Sectoral Allocation*

After defining the available financial resources the Development Board formulated investment plans on the basis of reports prepared by specialists on the different sectors of the economy. Thus flood control, irrigation and drainage projects formed the subject of detailed reports by a number of consultant firms, an industrial survey was undertaken, and the country's requirements for power, communication, etc., were studied by specialists. In addition, a few general studies were carried out by experts.[28] From these studies and reports a good picture of the requirements of the country could be drawn. Nevertheless a plan cannot be formulated by adding together every recommendation in the sectoral reports because total resources are limited.

The scale and timing of investment in each main sector were decided upon by the Development Board on the basis of its judgement after studying these reports, and its plans were no more than budgets for the allocation of oil revenues between different sectors.

FORMULATION OF GOVT. INVESTMENT PROGRAMMES 45

Inside a given sector there were a number of projects for each of which financial allocations were made every year—such as the industrial projects mentioned in Table III.2, and another group of projects for which financial allocations were made for the group as a whole—such as the projects mentioned in Table III.4. The plans consisted basically of a collection of projects and could not be related to possible increments in the national income since national income statistics only became available in 1958. The Development Board used simple common sense rather than formal methods of analysis in trying to avoid inconsistencies in its plans.

The Planning Board, on the other hand, tried to prepare investment programmes which were more sophisticated than those of the Development Board. The 1965–69 plan started by stating its aims which included improvement in the standard of living, economic unity between Arab States and redistribution of income in favour of poor classes.[29] To achieve these aims the planners fixed the compound rate of growth of income at 8% per annum (compared to 6.4% during 1953–63).[30] In order to achieve an overall growth rate of 8% planners decided to maintain the previous rate of growth of the industrial sectors, which was 12% per annum, raise the rate of growth of agriculture from zero to 7.5%, raise the rate of growth of other sectors slightly or maintain previous rates. The planners predicted the rate of growth of the so-called 'foreign oil sector' to be 6%.[31]

Given these desired rates of growth the increment to value added in each sector was calculated. Then these figures were multiplied by sectoral incremental capital–output ratios derived from Iraq's past experience or based on the experience of other countries similar to Iraq.

Table III.9 summarizes the process. Column 1 shows the

TABLE III.9

Investment Requirements of the Five-Year Plan, 1965–69

Sector	Value Added	I.D. Million Capital–Output Ratio	Investment
Agriculture	48	3·4	157
Industry	59	3·6	215
Transport	20	5·9	119
Other Sectors	101	3·3	330
Total	228	3·6	821

Source: Ministry of Guidance, Law No. 87 of 1965 for the Five-Year Economic Plan, 1965–69, p. 69

46 ROLE OF GOVERNMENT IN INDUSTRIALIZATION OF IRAQ

required value added in each sector, column 2 shows the sectoral capital–output ratios and column 3 the amount of investment required to bring about this increment in output.

The planners stated that in the past the share of the private sector in total investment was 50%, but due to nationalization in 1964 they expected this share to fall in the future and decided to raise the share of Government to 78% of the required amount of investment. Then the planners decided the shares of Government and the private investment in different sectors. For example, they argued that the additional I.D. 59 million of output in the industrial sector required I.D. 215 million of investment and expected the Government to invest I.D. 210 million, of which I.D. 168 was to come from the plan budget and I.D. 42 from other Government departments. This left I.D. 5 million to be invested by the private sector.[32]

Now, if the Development Board's approach to the allocation of available oil revenues among different sectors could be regarded as arbitrary in the sense that it was decided by common sense without the use of 'scientific' methods of analysis, the degree of arbitrariness was hardly reduced by the Planning Board's approach. The Planning Board's decision to aim at an 8% rate of growth (which in itself is a rate arbitrarily chosen) could be achieved by almost an indefinite combination of rates of growth of different sectors in the economy. The Planning Board arbitrarily decided upon one set of growth rates for each of the different sectors, but this choice determined at once the share of each sector in the Planning Board's total available funds, which could not be more than 50% of oil revenues. No one can seriously claim that one approach is more 'scientific' than the other, and no one can say which of the two methods can bring the system nearer to optimality.

In fact, all the six plans discussed consisted of no more than collections of projects chosen in a remarkably similar way despite the apparent difference in their shapes. Just as the Development Board's Technical Sections prepared sectoral plans that reflected the recommendations of expert reports, the Planning Board and the Ministry of Planning asked different Ministries to prepare their projects. Then each Ministry prepared its 'plan', i.e. its collection of projects, on the basis of previous plans and specialized reports. Added together these projects required larger amounts of funds than the planners expected to become available; therefore, some projects had to be cut by the Ministry of Planning and the Planning Board instead of by the old Ministry of Development and the Development Board.[33] The decisions on what projects to cut and what sectors to emphasize were determined by the general outlook

FORMULATION OF GOVT. INVESTMENT PROGRAMMES 47

of the Planning Board or the Development Board to economic development.

The pattern of allocation of funds among different sectors of the economy in the plans of the Development Board leaves no doubt that the chief aim was to develop agriculture by increasing land under utilization, increasing the productivity of land and introducing mechanization. In contrast, the plans of the Planning Board showed a marked shift in emphasis from agriculture to industry as can be seen from Table III.10 below.

TABLE III.10

Planned Distribution of Funds among Different Sectors 1951–65

Sector	Development Board			Planning Board		
	First Plan	Second Plan	Third Plan	Fourth Plan	Fifth Plan	Sixth Plan
Agriculture	42·6	37·6	33·5	12·2	20·3	25·9
Industry	20·0	14·3	13·4	9·8	29·9	28·0
Transport	19·8	24·4	24·9	25·7	24·5	16·4
Building	12·1	20·0	24·8	48·3	25·2	20·1
Other	5·5	3·7	3·4	3·6	0·0	9·6
Total	100·0	100·0	100·0	100·0	100·0	100·0

Source: Tables III.1 and III.5

Note: The Fourth plan does not include the projects of the Iraqi-Soviet agreement

The Development Board's emphasis on agriculture reflected the outlook of many reports submitted by specialists to the Government. These have pointed out that one of the major problems of Iraq was centred around the control of its water resources. The two rivers of Iraq, the Tigris and the Euphrates, often rise without warning and cause floods that damage irrigation works, plants, and property. They carry with them heavy sediments which silt up canals and barrages. Their water is slightly saline and when poured into the central and the southern plains the hot sun and high water table lead to salinization of the soil. They are at maximum flow too late for winter crops and too early for summer crops.[34]

It is clear, therefore, that flood control to prevent damage, and drainage to prevent salinization, were absolute necessities even if one did not want to extend the area under cultivation. By early 1956 two of the major flood control projects were completed and thereafter large amounts of the Euphrates flood water could be diverted into lake Habaniya and stored there, and the waters of the Tigris could be diverted into the Wadi Tharthar depression.

48   ROLE OF GOVERNMENT IN INDUSTRIALIZATION OF IRAQ

These two projects cost approximately I.D. 20 million, as compared with an estimated damage of I.D. 10 million inflicted by the 1954 flood alone. This might have been inflicted again in the spring of 1956 had these two projects not been completed.[35]

The majority of the population, however, depend for their livelihood on agriculture, but productivity per unit of land and per unit of labour is extremely low. Since a large proportion of population is on the land even if one allows for a moderate decline in the share of agriculture in the total labour force, a direct attack on the causes of low productivity in the agricultural sector was socially most desirable if by economic development one intends to improve the conditions of living of the majority of the population and guarantee cumulative growth. Agricultural development involves either a shift to summer crops on the existing farm lands, which requires additional water supply, or expansion of the cultivated area, which also requires additional water.

The flood control projects, which were desirable for the sake of flood control alone, could also provide additional water for irrigation. Since large areas of potentially cultivable land were available, a vast expansion of the agricultural sectors was therefore possible. Hence the Development Board was advised to emphasize agriculture in preference to industry. Thus the World Bank Mission stated that 'in a country like Iraq principal emphasis will inevitably need to be placed in the development of agriculture'.[36] Professor Iversen emphasized that fertile land was the most valuable asset of Iraq and the country 'has a large comparative advantage in agriculture, whereas the possibilities of creating new industries able to compete on equal terms with producers abroad are limited and more remote'.[37] Lord Salter shared these views and put forward a number of reasons why Iraq had no reason to emphasize industry: population pressure on land was small, there was no shortage of foreign exchange and in the long run the world's rapidly increasing population would press more and more upon food supplies; hence it is likely that the terms of trade would move in favour of agricultural countries.[38] He emphasized, however, that there would, and should, be industrialization 'beyond the present very modest limit'. He concluded that '(a) the amount of money to be devoted to industry should be on an altogether smaller scale than what is allotted to the support and expansion of agriculture, (b) the expansion so far as possible . . . should not outrun the available supplies of skilled labour . . . and (c) the industries should be carefully selected as being assured of a domestic market'.[39] The Little Report in recommending specific industrial projects applied the following criterion: 'The proposed industry must be able to produce

FORMULATION OF GOVT. INVESTMENT PROGRAMMES 49

at a cost below the landed price of comparable imported goods before import duty is levied . . . In the future it may be desirable to apply a less stringent test, but at the moment a number of industrial opportunities promise a profitability that does not need additional assistance. It is clearly desirable that they should be established first.'[40]

Table III.10, shows that all the plans of the Development Board followed the general development strategy suggested by experts and gave the highest priority to agriculture. Many observers have criticized this strategy for various reasons. Kanaan, for example, criticized the Development Board's strategy as a direct application of the Hecksher-Ohlin's version of the comparative cost theory which essentially is a static concept that ignores a variety of important dynamic elements.[41] Viner has demonstrated, however, that the comparative cost theory can be extended to incorporate dynamic elements such as changes in quantity and quality of factors of production, overtime, economies of scale, complementarity in producer and consumer markets etc.[42] This dynamic interpretation of the theory of comparative advantage means that scarce factors of today may become abundant in the future. It is not possible therefore to determine where the comparative advantage lies before making a comprehensive analysis of the possible changes in the supply of different factors of production in the future.

This clearly does not mean that the outcome of the analysis will emphasize industry. Nevertheless this type of analysis shows that the mechanical application of the comparative cost doctrine to a country like Iraq is likely to overemphasize agriculture and put severe restrictions on industrial expansion, such as that put forward by Lord Salter who recommended only industries based on local raw materials, assured of a domestic market and for which skills were available. If we wait for skills to come first, somehow, and then build factories to utilize the skilled labour, we may wait for a very long time indeed; this might not be wise because there is a physical limit to the expansion of agriculture.

In this respect it is interesting to notice that in 1952 a consultant firm made a technical and detailed survey of the utilization of agricultural resources in Iraq. This study pointed out that there is in the valley of the two rivers 22 million donums (one donum = 0.62 acres or 0.25 hectares) of arable and irrigable land, of which 13 million donums were then cultivated under the fallow system. Thus only another 9 million donums of land could ever be brought under cultivation.[43] A high income per worker in agriculture seems to require, among other things, a favourable land–agricultural

50   ROLE OF GOVERNMENT IN INDUSTRIALIZATION OF IRAQ

labour ratio, but this cannot be maintained, in the long run, in the face of ever increasing population unless a part of the growing population can be diverted into activities other than agriculture. Therefore other branches of economic activity, mainly industry, are needed to absorb at least a part of additional labour and capital.

Although the Development Board gave first priority to agriculture, it did not neglect industry and its plans during the period 1951–60 allocated I.D. 93 million to the industrial sector compared with the I.D. 4 millions total investment in modern industrial plants up to 1951.[44]

This however, did not satisfy the policy makers after the Revolution of July 1958. Thus the Fifth and Sixth Plans were formulated by the Planning Board and gave first priority to industry. Beside the alleged neglect of industry by the Development Board, it looks as if the Planning Board regarded industry as in some sense more productive than agriculture. Thus in an explanatory note to the Fifth Plan it was stated that 'industry increases national income by a higher percentage than agriculture with regard to capital and labour . . . while capital–output ratio was 8 for extensive cultivation in the Diala River Basin . . . it was estimated that capital output ratios were 3 or less in some industrial projects such as the glassware and the sulphur extraction projects'.[45]

Although it is reasonable to think that productivity per unit of capital and/or labour in a few industrial projects is higher than that of certain agricultural projects, it does not follow that productivity of additional capital will be higher in the industrial sector than in the agricultural sector. It is interesting to notice that the capital–output ratios of some state farms in the same plan were lower than those of the industrial projects mentioned above.[46] In the 1965–69 Five-Year Plan, the capital–output ratio of irrigation projects was estimated to be 5, but these are social overhead capital projects that make possible higher productivity elsewhere in the economy. The capital–output ratios for the whole agricultural sector in the plan was 3.4 compared to 3.6 for the industrial sector, including electricity.[47]

It should be remembered also that the definition of projects and sectors is, in the last analysis, arbitrary. Industrial projects, for example, are associated with urbanization, which requires more houses, schools, hospitals, power stations etc. Should some of the capital required by these projects be regarded as part of the capital cost of industrial projects or not? If one allows for these indirect capital requirements of industrialization, the capital–output ratio of this sector will become much higher. Therefore it is hard to conclude that the drastic shift in development strategy that took place after 1958 can be justified on the basis of capital–output ratios, even if we confine ourselves to information given in the plans.

Another justification for the shift of emphasis from agriculture to industry after 1958 seems to have been the Planning Board's belief that 'it is on the basis of industrial development that the economy progresses technically and the people acquire higher skills'.[48]

Although changes in productivity over time are important and the relative advantages of different sectors should therefore be measured over time, it does not follow that allowances for this factor will always favour industry. There is often as much scope for technical improvement in agriculture as in industry. The fact that most developed countries with high income per head have a large industrial sector in which productivity has been increasing may lead to the wrong conclusions if a comparison is made between this productivity and that of primitive agriculture in poor countries. If we look at the differences in productivity between developed and poor countries, we can see that there is often as much difference in the productivity of the agricultural sectors between developed and underdeveloped countries as in the industrial sectors.[49] The relevant comparison is between the two sectors in the same, or at least similar environments. This will narrow sharply, if not wipe out, the differences in productivity between the two sectors. The relevant thing is to compare the advantages of expansion and modernization of agriculture with industrial expansion, and not benefits of industrial development with horizontal expansion of primitive agriculture.

Our discussion of the arguments put forward by Iraqi policy makers and their advisers for emphasizing agriculture before, and industry after, 1958, was clearly inconclusive, since no satisfactory strategy can be derived from these theoretical discussions. It does not follow, however, that the allocation of resources among different sectors can not be dealt with systematically. In fact, proper assessment of costs and benefits derived at project, sub-sectoral and sectoral levels can go a long way towards producing a fairly satisfactory solution.

The trouble in Iraq has been the scarcity of well prepared projects or groups of interrelated projects ready for implementation. This is partly due to the lack of qualified specialists who can produce well planned desirable investment projects. Thus during the period of preparation of all the plans discussed, estimated available funds were much greater than the amount required for all the projects which were prepared and ready for implementation. Therefore one could not allocate all estimated available funds

52 ROLE OF GOVERNMENT IN INDUSTRIALIZATION OF IRAQ

among different sectors on the basis of well-studied projects. When dealing with projects which are not yet well analysed and ready for implementation, the problem of resource allocation becomes basically a matter of judgement, and there is no reason why even the most objective people should not have different opinions, especially if we remember that even the highly sophisticated arguments and theoretical reasoning designed for the far less difficult problem of choosing projects within each sector are inconclusive.

Even if there is a set of well prepared projects ready for implementation, one can rank them according to a variety of investment critera such as:

(a) the factor intensity criterion proposed by Polack and Buchanan,[50] according to which priority should be given to projects that use a minimum amount of the scarce factor of production. If capital is regarded as the scarce factor, priority should be given to projects with the lowest capital–output ratio. A special case of the factor intensity criterion is the so-called balance of payment criterion, which is concerned with the nature of the ultimate product. The criterion is that a sufficient portion of investment must fall into projects yielding additional exports or import-replacing goods to avoid balance of payment difficulties.

(b) The marginal social productivity criterion, as proposed by Khan and elaborated by Chenery,[51] states that efficient allocation is achieved by equating the marginal social productivity of any resource, including capital, in its various uses. To arrive at social marginal productivity Chenery suggested the application of a set of corrections to the businessman's calculation of the rate of profit to take care of external economies, use of idle resources, balance of payment situation, etc.

(c) The marginal reinvestment criterion, which was proposed by Galenson and Leibenstein,[52] is not concerned with maximization of the discounted value of the stream of income flow from any investment, but with the maximization of the stream of reinvestment from any investment project. Thus under certain restrained assumptions (i.e. that all wages are consumed and all profits are reinvested and that there is a direct relationship between capital intensity and labour productivity) this criterion recommends the choice of the most capital intensive alternative for any given amount of investable funds in order to maximize the rate of profit, which in turn will determine the rate of growth of the economy.

Each of these criteria has its own well known limitations and they lead to contradictory results. For example, the first criterion leads to projects with low capital–output ratio, while according to the third criterion planners are advised to concentrate on these projects

FORMULATION OF GOVT. INVESTMENT PROGRAMMES   53

or techniques of production with the highest capital intensity. As for the second criterion (social marginal productivity), it is clear that one can make any of the suggested corrections the decisive factor in determining the rank of projects by giving the parameter which represents that particular correction a sufficient value.

Under these circumstances the allocation of resources between different sectors can be best dealt with by a group of people who are aware of different aspects of the process of development and have a good knowledge of the country.[53] In Iraq members of such a group can hardly fulfil its functions if they are ministers, because cabinet changes are rapid and politicians are unlikely to have the required qualifications. Nor can a group of experts perform their basic function properly if they keep themselves occupied with the technical details of individual projects in the ways described in Chapter II above.

5. The Choice of Projects

We now turn to an analysis of the allocations of funds in the Iraqi plans for particular branches of industry or specific industrial projects.

The World Bank Mission in 1951 recommended that priority should be given to industries that would complement agriculture such as fertilizer, agricultural implements and processing of local agricultural commodities and to industries that would meet the growing local demand for consumer goods and construction material.[54] The Little report agreed with these views to a large extent, thus with the exception of the proposed steel rolling mill, all the recommended industries depended on local raw materials, particularly chemical resources.[55] Almost all the industries recommended in the report were designed to supply the domestic market, but the report stressed that this market was too small to justify a large industrial expansion based on chemical resources because even medium-sized plants would be fairly large in comparison with domestic consumption. Instead of arguing for the exploitation of chemical resources for the world market, the report recommended a number of small and medium-sized, but interrelated, industrial projects that had to be taken together if the programme was to be commercially successful on the basis of the local market.

The Development Board followed these general lines of advice and concentrated on the development of industries based on domestic resources and assured of a domestic market. Almost all the industrial projects of the Planning Board are also based on local raw materials and a domestic market. There are, however, a few exceptions, thus the rayon project will produce exclusively for the

E

54 ROLE OF GOVERNMENT IN INDUSTRIALIZATION OF IRAQ

domestic market, but beside domestic raw materials it will use certain imported raw materials to be produced locally in the future. The other important exception is the agricultural machinery plant which uses imported raw materials and has a capacity far larger than the local market needs.[56]

The 1965–69 five-year economic plan introduced two new allocation techniques; the use of criteria laid down by the United Nations in 'A Study of Industrial Growth' for allocating the total share of the industrial sector among subsectors,[57] and the use of particular 'priority ratios' in choosing specific projects.

Pattern of Industrial Growth

The United Nations study used the general analytical method of Chenery's 'Patterns of Industrial Growth',[58] and basic data for 53 countries in 1953 and 42 countries in 1958. The manufacturing sector was divided into 13 sub-sectors. Then by using the multiple regression method, the quantitative relations between the level of total manufacturing output and the output in each of the 13 sub-sectors, on the one hand, and per capita income and population on the other, were expressed in terms of a set of 'standard equations'. Given the size of the population and per capita income, the 'total manufacturing equation' will show the expected (or 'normal') size of the industrial sector for each country. Given the size of population, per capita income and the ratio of the actual to the calculated value of the industrial sector in each country, the set of 13 equations will give the expected ('normal') size of each sub-sector of the industrial sector in any country.[59]

The aim of the Sixth Plan was to increase national income by 8% per year and the continuation of the 12% rate of growth of the industrial sector. The planners estimated the level of national income, per capita income, and value added in the industrial sector for 1969 in constant 1956 prices. Applying the United Nations method to these macro-economic quantities Table III.11 was constructed. Column (1) shows value added in the manufacturing industrial sector after it was arranged from 17 to 13 sub-sectors. Column (2) shows how value added in this sector would have been distributed between different branches, had the pattern of industrial growth been similar to the so-called 'normal case' suggested in the U.N. study. Column (3) is the difference between the two columns and measures the amount of deviation from the 'normal' pattern. Column (4) shows the distribution of value added in 1969 by the application of the United Nations criterion.

Since it is too much to hope to obtain an industrial mix in complete conformity with the 'normal pattern' the planners divided

TABLE III.11

Growth of Industrial Branches Derived from the U.N. Pattern of Industrial Growth Technique

Industrial Sub-Sectors	Actual 1962 value added		Column 1 divided according to the U.N. criterion	1–2	1969 value added according to the U.N. criterion	1969 value added according to the 6th plan		Target Rates of Growth in the 6th Plan
	I.D. 000 1	%	2	3	4	I.D. 000 5	%	6
Food, Drink and Tobacco	19,650	34	22,668	− 3,018	41,404	38,386	30·0	10·0
Textiles	4,396	7·6	5,518	− 1,122	11,857	10,735	8·4	13·6
Clothing and Footwear	4,487	7·8	4,443	+ 044	9,593	9,637	7·6	11·5
Wood Products	1,442	2·5	3,136	− 1,694	7,418	5,724	4·5	21·8
Paper and its Products	145	0·3	789	− 644	2,482	1,838	1·4	43·7
Printing and Publishing	759	1·3	2,096	− 1,337	5,286	3,949	3·1	26·7
Leather Products	539	0·9	925	− 386	1,693	1,306	1·0	13·5
Rubber and Plastic Products	18	0·0	980	− 962	2,246	1,284	1·0	84·0
Chemical and Petroleum	12,639	21·8	5,030	+ 7,609	12,204	19,813	15·5	6·6
Non-metallic mineral products	8,669	15·0	4,282	+ 4,387	8,789	13,167	10·3	6·2
Metal products	440	0·8	882	− 442	3,004	2,562	2·0	28·6
Basic metals	3,510	6·1	6,293	− 2,783	19,668	16,885	13·2	25·6
Other Industries	1,134	1·9	775	+ 359	2,179	2,528	2·0	15·3
Total	57,817	100·0	57,817	12,389	127,823	127,823	100·0	12·0
Net National Product	503,130					862,160		8·0
Population, million	6·936					7·934		2·0
Per Capita Income I.D.	72·54					108·82		5·5
Value added in Industry as per cent of N.N.P.	10%					14·8%		

Source: Ministry of Planning: *The Five-Year Economic Plan*, 1965–69, p. 156

56 ROLE OF GOVERNMENT IN INDUSTRIALIZATION OF IRAQ

value added in 1969 between different branches of industry as shown in column (5). The items of this column were obtained by subtracting items of column (3) from those in column (4). This method implies a reduction in the amount of deviation between the country's industrial mix and the normal pattern. This is one alternative among a large number of possible adjustments. One can plan to increase the deviation or decrease it at various rates or simply to perpetuate it. The planners, however, chose to decrease the deviation, presumably because they regard this deviation as a sign of the immaturity of the economy.

By comparing columns (5) and (1) the rates of growth of all sub-sectors were calculated as shown in column (6). These rates were used, the planners claimed, to determine the amount of investment and the number of projects in each sub-sector.[60]

Since the industrial projects included in the 1965–69 plan were almost the same industrial projects as those in the previous plan,[61] it is safe to say that there was, in fact, no connection between the exercise based on the United Nations study and the actual selection of branches of industries and industrial projects. It was merely an exercise in 'scientific' planning. But we need not regret the absence of any such connection because the pattern of industrial growth assumed to be 'normal' by Chenery and the U.N. was hardly relevant to Iraq since it did not take account of trade or even of the endowment of resources such as oil.

It is interesting to notice that the application of the system of regression equations would give a high priority to sectors in which the country has no special advantage and a low priority to those branches in which the country has an obvious advantage. Thus if the requirements of Table III.11 are taken seriously, the lowest priority should go to chemicals and non-metallic minerals, while it is obvious that the country's supply of chemical raw materials and lack of metals and timber (instead of which bricks, tiles and cement are used widely) necessarily point in the other direction. According to the table, highest priority should be given to rubber, plastics, paper and wood products, but in most of these products Iraq has hardly any special advantage. The requirements of the table were not taken seriously and the plan gave highest priority to chemicals as Table III.8 shows.

Having failed to make any positive contribution, this type of analysis may nevertheless have had the effect of assuring the government that the projects were selected 'scientifically'. For example, even if it were true that a country like Iraq, in terms of population and per capita income, should have a larger industrial sector and should, therefore, push this sector, it would be unrealistic and

FORMULATION OF GOVT. INVESTMENT PROGRAMMES 57

unwise to argue on the basis of this analysis, that the so-called lagging branches, such as basic metallic products, should necessarily be established or enlarged. This type of approach could easily lead the Government to conclude that a project, such as the agricultural machinery project which was established under the Iraqi-Soviet agreement of 1959 to produce around 30,000 pieces of machinery for a market that can absorb only some 7,000 pieces, is a wise and 'scientific' choice! The country has neither a special advantage in producing these goods, nor the required raw materials, nor the market to absorb them.

Priority Ratios

The first five plans discussed did not specify the criteria used for the selection of projects. For the sixth plan, however, planners calculated the expected effects on the economy of the implementation of 17 of the 45 industrial projects included in the plan. On the basis of information supplied in the reports of consultant firms, planners calculated capital–output ratios, capital to foreign-exchange-saving ratios and capital–labour ratios. These ratios are given in table III.12. The planners pointed out that projects which produce more output per unit of capital expenditure are preferred to projects with higher capital–output ratio, and projects that save more foreign exchange per unit of investment are better than those with a higher capital to foreign exchange ratio, while projects which employ more unskilled labour per unit of investment are preferred to those that employ less.[62]

Although it is possible to rank projects according to any of these criteria, and obtain specific results, it is extremely difficult to use more than one criteria unless accepted rates of substitution between the criteria are specified. It is necessary to decide that x units of output have the same desirability as y units of saving foreign exchange and z units of unskilled labour employed. The planners, however, did not specify their objectives in these terms, they only stated vaguely that they had used these ratios to decide the priority of projects. But since all the 17 industrial projects were included in the previous plan, it is hard to say that there was any relationship between these priority ratios and the inclusion of these projects in the sixth plan.

In summary, the policy in choosing projects was to concentrate on those projects that used local raw materials and found an outlet for their product in the domestic market. In the 1965–69 plan, the planners stated that at a later stage emphasis would be put on the exploitation of local petrochemical raw materials for the world market.[63] It seems that within these general lines of policy any

58 ROLE OF GOVERNMENT IN INDUSTRIALIZATION OF IRAQ

TABLE III.12

Priority Ratios in the Sixth Plan, 1965–69:
The Industrial Sector—Selected Projects

Project	Gross Capital–Output Ratio	Net Capital–Output Ratio	Capital to Foreign-Exchange-Saving Ratio	Capital–Labour Ratio
	1	2	3	4
Kut Cotton Textile	4·0	5·2	3·8	5·0
Hilla Rayon Textile	4·1	5·1	3·6	3·8
Expansion of Mosul Cotton Textile	3·0	3·7	2·8	4·0
Kut Stocking and Underwear Project	2·0	2·3	1·5	2·0
Basrah Paper Plant	6·3	9·1	11·3	18·8
Samara Antibiotic Project	4·5	5·6	3·6	7·3
Hindiya Rayon Project	11·5	47·6	10·8	15·0
Kirkuk Sulphur Extraction Plant	4·0	}		
Basrah Fertilizer Plant	5·0	}	10·0	15·0
Four different Petro-chemical plants	6·0	}		
Natural Gas Pipeline	4·0	4·6	negative	155·0
Basrah Refinery	3·7	4·3	negative	15·0
Ramadi Glass Plant	5·2	7·7	5·3	3·7
Ramadi Ceramic Project	1·9	2·1	2·9	2·4
Iron and Steel Project	6·0		10·0	15·0
Electrical Equipment Project— Baghdad	3·2	4·0	3·5	2·7
Agricultural Machinery Plant	5·8	7·9	8·9	4·1
Total	4·9			8·7

Source: Ministry of Planning, *Five-Year Economic Plan, 1965–69*, pp. 237, 243 and 245

single industrial project was tested by its commercial profitability. But this does not mean that consistent methods were used to arrive at proper costs and benefits. In fact, the prices of outputs and inputs used were sometimes unadjusted for things like custom duties and in some cases the local *market* prices of imported goods were compared with the *cost* of local production in order to arrive at the rates of profit from capital investment in industrial projects.

Thus, the feasibility study of the Nassiriah Woollen Textile project,[64] compared the cost of production of the proposed mill with the Baghdad market price of imported woollen textiles, and the project showed a 15% profit on capital. Nowhere in the report were import duties mentioned. The local market price of imported woollen textiles includes 35% import duties and the profit margin

FORMULATION OF GOVT. INVESTMENT PROGRAMMES 59

of the importer and the wholesaler, and these profits are likely to be inflated because imports were subject to a quota system.[65] The point is that one cannot rank projects according to their profitability if the set of prices used in estimating profits are not consistent. If costs of domestic production are not compared with landed price of imported goods before duties are levied, the duty rates will become the decisive factor in ranking projects according to their profitability. Since tariff rates are arbitrarily imposed and changed by the Government, it is clear that they do not bear any relationship to real costs and benefits. Therefore they must be excluded in this type of study.

Professor Arthur Lewis once pointed out that 'the quality and the forms of plans should be limited strictly within the capacity of the machine'.[66] In Iraq the planning machinery did not apply the simple commercial profitability test in a consistent manner, nevertheless, it tried to use more delicate methods such as national income, balance of payment and employment tests in the formulation of the 1965–69 plan. As a result this plan was an impressive document in comparison with the previous plans, but, as we have shown in this chapter, the difference between it and previous plans was illusory. Moreover, some of the techniques used in the formulation of it could have regrettable consequences for the economy if taken seriously.

REFERENCES

1. See Table 1.3
2. The Industrial Bank, May 1965, *Report*, p. 10
3. Langley, *Industrialization of Iraq*, p. 207
4. Qubain, *Reconstruction of Iraq*, pp. 169–172
5. I.B.R.D., *Economic Development of Iraq*, p. 37
6. Lord Salter, *The Development of Iraq*, pp. 218–19
7. al-Khalaf, *The Economic, Physical and Human Geography of Iraq*, p. 280
8. Lord Salter, *The Development of Iraq*, p. 7
9. Langley, *Industrialization of Iraq*, p. 206
10. Qubain, *Reconstruction of Iraq*, p. 43
11. Development Board and Ministry of Development Law No. 43, 1955 of the Second Plan, p. 8
12. Arthur D. Little, *A Plan for Industrial Development in Iraq*, pp. 377–89
13. *Ibid.*, pp. 18–19
14. The Development Board and Ministry of Development, Law No. 54, 1956 of the Third Plan, 1955–60, p. 3
15. Law No. 54, 1956 of the Third Plan, pp. 26–9
16. Ministry of Guidance, Law No. 181 of 1959 for the provisional Economic Plan, pp. 81–2
17. Law No. 52 of 1959 for the Economic and Technical Agreement between the Republic of Iraq and the Union of Soviet Socialist Republics, reprinted in Hassan, *Studies in Economics of Iraq*, pp. 417–40
18. Langley, *Industrialization of Iraq*, pp. 268–269

60 ROLE OF GOVERNMENT IN INDUSTRIALIZATION OF IRAQ

19. The Tobacco Monopoly was established in 1939 to improve the quality of tobacco, to assure farmers stable and reasonable prices and to raise revenue. See I.B.R.D., *Economic Development of Iraq*, p. 26
20. Hassan, *Studies in Economics of Iraq*, p. 267
21. The Board received its share of oil revenue in foreign exchange. It used some of this to purchase foreign materials. The remainder was sold to the Central Bank for Iraqi Dinars and the Board used them to purchase local labour and material. Those whose income is increased directly or indirectly in the process of development spend part of their extra income on imported goods. From the point of view of the economy the importance of the foreign exchange is that it enables the country to finance these imports and this prevents, or at least modifies, the inflationary effects of the development process
22. For a discussion of the optimum investment ratio, see Sen *On Optimizing the Rate of Saving*; and Horvat, *The Optimum Rate of Investment*
23. Ministry of Guidance Laws, Nos. 70, 1961, p. 68; 87, 1965, p. 50
24. Assuming a low capital–output ratio of 3·5, as compared with 4 to 5 in the past, this target might have been met by investing I.D. 580 million during 1961–65 by the Government. During the same period total oil revenues were I.D. 556 million. See Ministry of Guidance, Law No. 70, 1961, pp. 67–8 and table I.6, p. 11
25. Almost 70% of funds to finance the 1961–65 plan was expected to come from oil revenues and foreign loans. Out of the remaining 30%, 25% was a deficit to be obtained somehow and almost 80% of the remaining 5% to come from the Port Administration, which raised duty per ton on exported oil. A rise in exports was also anticipated. See Ministry of Guidance Law No. 70, 1961, pp. 71, 73 and Law No. 87, 1965, p. 49
26. The Ministry of Planning tried to increase the share of oil revenues devoted to capital formation from 50% to 60% but it failed. See Ministry of Guidance Law No. 70, 1961, p. 70 and Law No. 87 1965, p. 49
27. See Tables I.16 and IV.8 and Hashim, *Capital Formation in Iraq, 1957–62*, p. 216
28. The General Reports were the I.B.R.D., Report, *op. cit.*, Lord Salter's Report *op. cit.*, and Professor Iverson, *A Report on Monetary Policy in Iraq*. For a list of sectoral reports see Salter, *op. cit.*, pp. 244–7
29. Ministry of Guidance, Law No. 87, 1965, pp. 50–1
30. *Ibid.*, p. 54
31. *Ibid.*, p. 59
32. *Ibid.*, p. 68
33. Development Board and Ministry of Development, Law No. 43, 1955, p. 1 and Ministry of Guidance Law No. 70, 1961, p. 63
34. Development Board, *Development of the Tigris–Euphrates Valley*, pp. 1, 6 and 13
35. Langley, *Industrialization of Iraq*, p. 120
36. I.B.R.D., *Economic Development of Iraq*, p. 97
37. Iversen, *Monetary Policy of Iraq*, p. 177
38. Slater, *The Development of Iraq*, p. 17
39. *Ibid.*, p. 18
40. Little, *A Plan for Industrial Development in Iraq*, p. 9
41. Kanaan, T. H. *Input–Output and Social Accounts of Iraq*, Chapter II, p. 14
42. Viner, J., *Stability and Progress: The Poorer Countries' Problem*, pp. 61–2
43. The Development Board, *Development of the Tigris–Euphrates Valley*, p. 4
44. I.B.R.D., *Economic Development of Iraq*, p. 33
45. Ministry of Guidance, Law No. 70, 1961, p. 78
46. *Ibid.*, pp. 208–16

FORMULATION OF GOVT. INVESTMENT PROGRAMMES   61

47. Ministry of Guidance, Law No. 87, 1965, p. 69
48. Ministry of Planning, *Report on the Draft Broad Lines for the Detailed Economic Plan*, quoted by Kanaan, *Input–Output and Social Accounts of Iraq*, Chapter II, p. 14
49. Clark, *Conditions of Economic Progress*, pp. 276, 236
50. Polak, J., *Balance of Payments Problems of Countries Reconstructing with Help of Foreign Loans*, pp. 208–32 and Buchanan, N., *International Investment and Domestic Welfare*, pp. 24, 72, 106–8
51. Kahn, A. E., *Investment Criteria in Development Programmes*, pp. 38–61 and Chenery, H. B., *The Application of Investment Criteria*, pp. 76–96
52. Galenson, W., and Leibenstein, H., *Investment Criteria, Productivity and Economic Development*, pp. 343–76
53. Tinbergen, *The Relevance of Theoretical Criteria in Selection of Investment Plans*, p. 10
54. I.B.R.D., *Economic Development of Iraq*, pp. 35–8, 53
55. Langley, *Industrialization of Iraq*, p. 219
56. Ministry of Guidance, Law No. 70, 1961, for the 1961–65 plan, p. 295, and information provided by Mr. H. K. al-Duri, Engineer in the metallic industries section of the Department of Industrial Design and Construction, Ministry of Industry
57. United Nations, Department of Economic and Social Affairs, *A Study of Industrial Growth*
58. Chenery, *Patterns of Industrial Growth*, pp. 624–51
59. United Nations, *A Study of Industrial Growth*, pp. 6, 32
60. Ministry of Planning, *The Five-Year Economic Plan, 1965–69*, p. 154
61. Compare Tables III.7 and III.8 and see pp. 41–42
62. Ministry of Planning, *The Five-Year Economic Plan, 1965–69*, pp. 239–40
63. *Ibid.*, p. 247
64. Ministry of Industry, *The Feasibility Study of the Nassiriah Woollen Textile Project*
65. The quota system is discussed in Chapter VI.
66. Lewis, A., *Principles of Economic Planning*, p. 122

Chapter IV

IMPLEMENTATION OF GOVERNMENT INVESTMENT PROGRAMMES: 1951–65

The aim of this chapter is to discuss implementation of investment programmes, to show how far plan targets were achieved and analyse how far the reorganization of the planning machinery in 1959 improved the process of implementation. For this purpose the period is subdivided into two periods, the first being 1951–58, during which the Development Board formulated and implemented investment plans, and the second being 1959–65, during which the Planning Board formulated investment programmes and the operating ministries were responsible for plan implementation.

1. *The Experience of Implementation*

While the formulation of a consistent plan is indisputably necessary, what matters more is its implementation. Failure to carry out plans may manifest itself in different ways, such as failure to invest in economically sound projects, delays in the execution of projects, inferior construction, selection of low-yield projects and inability to use facilities provided by investment.[1]

Unfortunately data reflecting the implementation of development plans in Iraq are fragmentary. Except for investment figures no adequate information is available. Moreover, up to the sixth plan 1965–69, the plans did not contain adequate overall or sectoral targets for national income, employment, balance of payments etc., against which to appraise them.

Overemphasis on financial investment targets can be regarded as a sign of bad planning which may have detrimental repercussions because it tends to focus attention on the fulfilment of the financial rather than on the real targets of investment, which are physical. This, as Reddaway has pointed out, is 'to mistake the means for the objective, the fundamental objective of the plan is to obtain the higher level of output'.[2] On the other hand the value of capital formation that results from investment depends on how and where money is invested. It is not inconceivable that large sums of money may be invested in projects that serve no useful purpose. Moreover, some items of current expenditure on health and education

IMPLEMENTATION OF GOVT. INVESTMENT PROGRAMMES   63

may be more productive in the long run than much of the investment in magnificent public buildings, boulevards, uneconomic industrial projects, expensive housing for the bureaucracy, etc., even though neither can be quantified. Nevertheless, we shall examine the implementation of Iraq's plans with reference to actual expenditure, simply because of lack of information, and because financial expenditures were the main targets of the plans. Under these circumstances a proper measure of plan implementation is the extent to which the investment targets of the plans were achieved.

TABLE IV.1

Planned Investment, Actual Capital Expenditure and Total Revenues of the Development Programmes, 1951–65

I.D. Millions

Year	Planned Investment	Actual Investment	Revenue devoted to Plans	2 as % of 1	2 as % of 3	3 as % of 1
	1	2	3	4	5	6
1951	9·3	3·1	7·4	33·3	41·8	79·5
1952	20·5	7·8	23·9	38·0	32·6	116·6
1953	28·4	12·3	35·2	43·3	34·9	123·9
1954	31·5	20·9	40·7	66·3	51·3	129·2
1955	46·6	32·0	60·7	68·6	52·7	130·2
1956	81·9	43·0	51·1	52·5	84·1	62·4
1957	100·8	57·4	35·8	56·9	160·3	35·5
1958	99·5	52·2	61·7	52·4	84·6	62·0
1959	80·0	49·9	43·5	62·4	114·7	54·4
1960	143·0	47·5	47·6	33·2	99·7	33·3
1961	97·1	60·8	66·6	62·6	91·2	68·6
1962	108·0	58·7	70·0	54·3	83·8	64·8
1963	117·6	53·5	67·6	45·4	79·1	57·5
1964	119·6	74·0	76·4	61·8	96·8	66·3
1965	123·2	57·1	70·8	46·3	80·6	57·4
1951–58	418·8	228·7	316·9	54·6	72·2	75·6
1959–65	788·5	401·5	442·5	50·9	90·7	56·1
1951–65	1,207·3	630·2	759·4	52·2	82·9	62·9

Source: Law No. 181 of 1959, p. 11; Law No. 70 of 1961, p. 11; Law No. 54 of 1956, p. 11; Law No. 87 of 1965, p. 72; Central Bank of Iraq, *Quarterly Bulletin*, No. 59, p. 46; Central Bank of Iraq, *Bulletin, New Series*, No. 3, 1967, pp. 28–29; No. 4, 1967, pp. 28–29

Note: Column (2) excludes administrative expenditures of the Development Board and all loans. Revenue for 1965 is provisional

Expenditure–Allocation Ratio: This ratio shows the relationship between planned investment and actual investment, i.e. between goals and achievements. The higher the ratio the more successful has been the plan in carrying out its investment target. The first column of Table IV.1 shows that allocation of funds for investment was rising; it increased from less than I.D. 10 million in 1951 to

64 ROLE OF GOVERNMENT IN INDUSTRIALIZATION OF IRAQ

I.D. 123.2 million in 1965. Actual expenditure was moderate at the beginning, but it started to rise rapidly during the first period 1951–58; it increased from I.D. 3.1 million in 1951 to I.D. 57.4 million in 1957, the momentum was then lost and the 1965 level of I.D. 57.1 is almost equal to the 1957 level.

A comparison between columns (1) and (2) of Table IV.1, shows that expenditure was always less than planned investment. The ratio of expenditure to allocation, given in column (4) of the same table, was 52% for the whole period, but the ratio was higher in the first period. Moreover, during 1951–58 the ratio rose from the low level of 33% to 52% in 1958, but during the second period the ratio fell to 46% in 1965. Thus while the gap between promise and achievement was narrowing during the Development Board period, it appears to have widened during the Planning Board's period.

Expenditure–Revenue Ratio: Planners may exaggerate revenues hence actual investment will be less than planned expenditure. Column (3) of Table IV.1 shows that revenues were rising rapidly during the first period with the exception of 1956–57, when revenues dropped sharply due to the blowing up of the oil pipelines in Syria during the Suez crisis of 1956.[3] At the beginning of the second period revenues dropped again due to the Revolutionary Government's decision to decrease the percentage of oil revenues devoted to the development plans from 70% to 50%.[4] Column (5) of Table IV.1 shows that the ratio of expenditure to revenues was 41% in 1951 but rose to 84% by 1958. At the end of the same year accumulated funds, despite the Suez crisis, were I.D. 84.6 million. During the second period the ratio increased to 90%, compared with 72% during the first period. This improvement, was mainly the result of a fall and stagnation in revenues rather than of increased expenditure. Throughout the whole period, however, there was a marked inability to spend available funds.

Sectoral Underspending: Table IV.2 shows the ratio of actual expenditure to planned investment in the four major sectors. It shows that throughout the period 1951–65 the achievement of investment targets was the lowest in the industrial sector. Compared with an overall ratio of actual investment to planned investment of 52%, the ratio was only 40% for the industrial sector. It is interesting that the situation of the industrial sector did not improve during the second period. In fact the ratio fell from 46% during 1951–58 to 38% during 1959–65. Thus the gap between goals and achievements of the industrial sector increased during the Planning Board period. Moreover, whereas the ratio improved from 3.3% in 1952 to 108% in 1958, it decreased to 47% in 1965.

Table IV.3 shows that the Development Board gave first priority

TABLE IV.2

Actual Expenditure by Sectors as % of Annual Sectoral Allocation, 1951–65

	1951	1952	1953	1954	1955	1956	1957	1958	1959	1960	1961	1962	1963	1964	1965	1951 –58	1959 –65	1951 –65
Agriculture	34·0	33·0	47·3	71·1	82·2	45·5	49·6	42·7	68·6	54·0	48·7	31·1	19·7	27·1	23·5	51·1	36·6	43·8
Industry	0·0	3·3	10·0	33·3	21·9	29·4	53·7	108·1	48·0	40·7	48·6	41·8	23·9	38·3	47·0	46·2	38·7	40·8
Communication	28·5	44·7	40·4	81·1	59·5	51·9	42·3	24·6	54·7	21·3	56·8	48·7	61·4	67·3	46·7	42·6	49·6	47·1
Building	25·7	80·6	75·6	76·9	77·6	81·6	80·2	73·9	69·3	32·5	79·2	85·6	83·4	133·3	60·0	76·4	68·5	70·8
All Sectors	33·3	38·0	42·8	66·3	68·6	52·5	56·9	52·4	62·3	33·2	62·6	54·3	45·4	61·8	46·3	54·6	50·9	52·1

Source: Derived from Tables IV.3 and IV.4

TABLE IV.3

Sectoral Distribution of Planned Investment, 1951–65

I.D. Million

Year	Agriculture 1		Industry 2		Communication 3		Building 4		Total 5
	I.D.	%	I.D.	%	I.D.	%	I.D.	%	I.D.
1951	4·7	45·6	0·0	0·0	2·1	20·4	3·5	33·9	10·3
1952	10·6	51·7	3·0	14·6	3·8	18·5	3·1	15·1	20·5
1953	15·0	52·9	5·0	17·6	4·7	16·6	3·7	12·8	28·4
1954	16·3	51·7	6·0	19·0	5·3	16·8	3·9	12·3	31·5
1955	14·1	30·2	4·1	8·7	14·1	30·2	14·3	30·6	46·6
1956	27·0	32·9	17·0	20·7	17·7	21·6	20·2	24·6	81·9
1957	26·6	26·3	16·0	15·8	29·3	29·0	28·9	28·6	100·8
1958	29·5	29·6	11·0	11·0	32·1	32·2	26·9	27·0	99·5
1959	15·0	18·7	10·0	12·5	23·0	28·7	32·0	40·0	80·0
1960	20·0	14·1	14·0	9·8	37·0	26·0	71·0	50·0	142·0
1961	19·7	20·3	14·4	14·8	24·8	25·6	38·0	39·7	96·9
1962	20·2	18·7	24·7	22·8	32·4	30·0	30·7	28·4	108·0
1963	22·8	19·3	39·6	33·6	29·8	25·3	25·4	21·5	117·6
1964	24·7	20·6	43·0	35·9	27·9	23·3	24·0	20·0	119·6
1965	25·1	20·3	32·1	26·0	26·5	21·5	39·5	32·6	123·2
1951–58	143·8	34·3	62·1	14·8	109·1	26·0	104·5	24·9	419·5
1959–65	147·5	18·7	177·8	22·5	201·4	25·5	260·6	33·1	787·3
1951–64	291·3	24·1	239·9	19·8	310·5	25·7	365·1	30·2	1,206·8

Source: Central Bank of Iraq, *Annual Report*, 1963, p. 217, and 1965, p. 351; Law No. 87 of 1965, p. 72; Law No. 181 of 1959, p. 11; Law No. 70 of 1961, p. 11; Central Bank of Iraq, *Bulletin, New Series*, No. 3, 1967, p. 29 and No. 4, 1967, p. 29

TABLE IV.4

Sectoral Actual Investment as % of Total Investment, 1951–65

I.D. Million

Year	Agriculture 1 I.D.	%	Industry 2 I.D.	%	Communication 3 I.D.	%	Building 4 I.D.	%	Total 5 I.D.
1951	1·6	51·6	0·0	0·0	0·6	19·3	0·9	29·0	3·1
1952	3·5	44·8	0·1	1·2	1·7	21·8	2·5	32·1	7·8
1953	7·1	57·7	0·5	4·1	1·9	15·4	2·8	22·7	12·3
1954	11·6	55·5	2·0	9·5	4·3	20·5	3·0	14·3	20·9
1955	11·6	36·2	0·9	2·8	8·4	26·2	11·1	34·7	32·0
1956	12·3	28·6	5·0	11·6	9·2	21·3	16·5	38·4	43·0
1957	13·2	21·9	8·6	15·0	12·4	21·6	23·2	40·4	57·4
1958	12·6	24·1	11·9	22·7	7·9	15·1	19·9	38·0	52·3
1959	10·3	20·6	4·8	9·6	12·6	25·2	22·2	44·4	49·9
1960	10·8	22·7	5·7	12·0	7·9	16·6	23·1	48·6	47·5
1961	9·6	15·7	7·0	11·5	14·1	23·1	30·1	49·5	60·8
1962	6·3	10·7	10·3	17·5	15·8	26·9	26·3	44·8	58·7
1963	4·5	8·4	9·5	17·7	18·3	34·2	21·2	39·6	53·5
1964	6·7	9·0	16·5	22·2	18·8	25·4	32·0	43·2	74·0
1965	5·9	10·3	15·1	26·4	12·4	21·7	23·7	41·5	57·1
1951–58	73·5	32·1	29·0	12·6	46·4	20·0	79·9	34·9	228·7
1959–65	54·1	13·5	68·9	17·1	99·9	24·9	178·6	44·4	401·5
1951–65	127·6	20·3	97·9	15·6	146·3	23·3	254·5	41·1	626·3

Source: Central Bank of Iraq: *Annual Report*, 1963, p. 218; *Quarterly Bulletin*, No. 59, p. 47, *Bulletin, New Series*, No. 3, 1967, p. 29 and No. 4, 1967, p. 29

Note: Expenditure excludes administrative expenditure of the Development Board, and all loans and transfer of funds to the ordinary budget.

68 ROLE OF GOVERNMENT IN INDUSTRIALIZATION OF IRAQ

to agriculture and devoted 14.8% of planned investment to industry. Although the Planning Board gave first priority to industry,[5] this is not reflected in Table IV.3, because planned investment in this sector did not include the cost of machinery and equipment that was expected to be provided by the Soviet Union according to the Iraqi-Soviet Technical and Economic Co-operation Agreement, for the years 1959–60; also the Fourth and Fifth Plans were terminated before their whole period was over and these plans concentrated industrial investment in the final years.

Table IV.4 shows the distribution of actual investments between different sectors. It shows that the ratio of investment in agriculture to total investment decreased from 32% during 1951–58 to only 14% during 1959–65. The sharp decline in the share of agriculture in total investment did not result, however, in any significant improvement in the share of industry, because the ratio of investment in industry to total investment increased only from 13% during the first period to 17% during the second period. The largest share of the investment went to the public buildings sector and the ratio of investment in building to total investment increased from 34% during the Development Board period to 44% during the Planning Board period. The combined share of agriculture and industry fell from 45% to 31% between the two periods. Thus although the Planning Board justified its relative neglect of agriculture by the necessity of shifting emphasis to industry,[6] it in fact turned out to emphasize public buildings not industry.

Table IV.5 shows that during the period 1951–65 there was a marked deviation of the actual pattern of investment from the planned composition of capital expenditure. Thus although 19.8% of funds were devoted to industry only 15.5% of actual investment went to this sector. While 41% of funds were invested in public buildings, 30% was devoted to this sector in the plans. The table

TABLE IV.5

Deviation of Actual Pattern of Expenditure from
Planned Composition of Investment, 1951–65
%

	1951–58		1959–65		1951–65	
Sector	*Planned*	*Actual*	*Planned*	*Actual*	*Planned*	*Actual*
Agriculture	34·3	32·2	18·7	13·5	24·2	20·2
Industry	14·8	12·6	22·5	17·1	19·8	15·5
Communication	26·0	20·3	25·5	24·9	25·7	23·2
Buildings	24·9	34·9	33·3	44·5	30·3	41·1
Total	100·0	100·0	100·0	100·0	100·0	100·0

Source: Derived from Tables IV.3 and IV.4

also shows that during the Planning Board period the pattern of actual investment deviated more from the planned pattern of investment than it did during the Development Board period. This means that the plans of the Development Board governed actual expenditure to a larger degree than the plans of the Planning Board. In other words the implementation process upset the priorities of the Development Board to a smaller degree than those of the Planning Board. This indicates a setback in the quality of the planning process.

Thus during the period 1951–65, implementation failure manifests itself in a marked inability to use available funds in economically sound projects, a large and increasing gap between promise and achievement, while priorities outlined in the plans were distorted by the implementation process.

2. *The Main Causes of Failure.*

Poor plan implementation may be attributed to a combination of administrative ineffiency, over-ambitious plans, technical and political factors.

Ambitious Plans: Out of the six plans, covering the period 1951–65, five were unduly ambitious even in the strict sense of financial requirements. Column (6) of Table IV.1 shows that during 1951–65 actual revenues came to only 63% of planned investment. During the early part of 1951–58 period, planners underestimated revenues while during the latter part of the same period there was an obvious overestimation of revenues aggravated by the Suez crisis of 1956. Overestimation of revenues increased by far during the 1959–65 period, thus while the ratio of revenue to planned investment was 63% for the whole period, it was only 56% for the 1959–65 period compared to 75% during 1951–58. Thus even if all available revenues were utilized, actual investment would have been equal to 75% of planned investment in the first period and only 56% during the second period. This means that planners, especially during the second period, overestimated the political will of the Government to develop and hence overestimated the amount of funds that the Government was prepared to devote to capital formation.

Overestimation of revenues has many unfavourable consequences. Thus the plans will tend to include beside a number of much needed projects many less essential and dubious schemes, consequently the investment programme may move in all directions at the same time. But because of physical and administrative as well as financial limitations, implementation will be slow; this means that large amounts of funds may be immobilized in many projects from which little benefit can be derived over the short run. More-

F

70 ROLE OF GOVERNMENT IN INDUSTRIALIZATION OF IRAQ

over, overestimation of revenues tends to upset the pattern of planned investment.

To show the effect of overestimated revenues on the relationship between the pattern of planned investment and the composition of actual expenditure, I have distributed actual revenues of the plans during 1959–65 among different sectors according to the priorities of the plan. Thus in row 2a of Table IV.6 actual revenues during the period, which were I.D. 442 million, are distributed between different sectors according to actual plan priorities given in row 1b of the same Table.

TABLE IV.6

Distribution of Actual Revenue between Sectors according to Priorities of the 1959–65 Plan

I.D. Millions

		Agriculture	*Industry*	*Communications*	*Building*	*Total*
1. Planned Investment on the	a. I.D.	147·4	177·8	201·4	260·6	787·2
basis of estimated revenues	b. %	18·7	22·5	25·6	33·1	100·0
2. Planned Investment on the	a. I.D.	84·0	100·0	112·0	146·0	442·0
basis of actual revenue	b. %	19·0	22·6	25·3	33·0	100·0
3. Actual Investment	a. I.D.	54·1	68·9	99·9	178·6	401·5
	b. %	13·4	17·2	24·9	44·5	100·0
4. Actual Investment with no	a. I.D.	54·1	68·9	99·9	146·0	368·9
shift of funds between	b. %	14·7	18·7	27·1	39·5	100·0
Sectors						

Source: Derived from Tables IV.1, IV.3 and IV.4

In row 4a we show what the amount of investment would have been in each sector, had planned investment, given in row 2a, set a ceiling on actual investment in each sector. The only sector which is affected in this way is the public buildings sector, in which investment is reduced from I.D. 178.6 million to I.D. 146.0 million. Had the planning process worked in this manner an extra amount of I.D. 22.5 million would have been added to unutilized funds. The point is not whether it is or is not desirable to invest money in public buildings rather than keeping it to be invested in other sectors in the future; what I want to emphasize here is that exaggerated estimates of revenues tend to upset the pattern of planned expenditure and this has occurred in Iraq. The results of Table IV.6 are summarized in Table IV.7. This table shows that the degree of deviation between the actual pattern of expenditure and the planned composition of

IMPLEMENTATION OF GOVT. INVESTMENT PROGRAMMES 71

investment would have been less had the planners not exaggerated revenues. But unrealistic targets are only one reason among many more serious reasons which cause underspending and tend to upset the planned pattern of investment.

TABLE IV.7

Overestimated Revenues and the Deviation of the Actual Pattern of Investment from the Planned Pattern, 1959–65
%

Sector	Planned and Actual Investment on the Basis of Estimated Revenues %		Planned and Actual Investment on the Basis of Actual Revenues %	
	Planned	Actual	Planned	Actual
Agriculture	18·6	14·1	18·6	15·0
Industry	22·5	17·0	22·5	19·0
Communication	25·5	24·9	25·5	27·0
Buildings	33·4	44·0	33·4	39·0
Total	100·0	100·0	100·0	100·0

Source: Derived from Table IV.6

Administrative inefficiency: Successful plan implementation depends 'on the technical competence and integrity of the administration',[7] because implementation is largely a matter of proper organization and administration. We have demonstrated in Chapter II that the administrative machinery of the Iraqi Government was not geared to the exceptionally large spending made possible by oil revenues. The administration was characterized by excessive centralization, low morale, lack of co-ordination and lack of a sufficient sense of urgency. We have also mentioned that promotion was based on seniority and other considerations rather than merit. Officials were frequently shifted from one position to another without regard to their experience and they did not stay in one department long enough to become really useful, there were also serious defects in the paper work, registry, and archives. All these defects seriously affected the efficiency of the administration yet little systematic attention was paid to administrative improvements.

After the Revolution of July 1958 Government recurrent expenditure increased vastly as can be seen from column (2) of Table IV.8. Such a development is bound to have favourable effects on a country's capacity to absorb capital expenditure provided that emphasis is put on the expansion of those departments which are directly concerned with plan formulation and implementation, such as Ministries of Industry and Planning, and even departments of health and education, which can indirectly increase the absorption capacity of the economy in the long run.

72 ROLE OF GOVERNMENT IN INDUSTRIALIZATION OF IRAQ

Table IV.9 shows the main elements of the Government's ordinary budget expenditure during 1951–65. Column (4) shows that during the first period current expenditure of the departments concerned with plan implementation increased very slowly from I.D. 0.9 million in 1951 to I.D. 2.9 million in 1958 representing 2.9% and 3.6% of total ordinary expenditure. During the second period 1959–65, expansion was also slow and the current expenditure of the planning administration (i.e. departments concerned with plan formulation and implementation) increased to I.D. 3.6 million in 1963. Moreover, the ratio of current expenditure on the planning machinery to total ordinary expenditure decreased from 3.7% on average during the first period to 2.6% during 1959–63.[8] Column (3) of Table IV.9, however, shows that there was a significant expansion in expenditure on health and education, but that this was overshadowed by the great expansion in expenditure on security and defence. For example, expenditure on health and education

TABLE IV.8

A Comparison between Government Capital Expenditure, Current Expenditure and National Income

I.D. Millions

Year	Capital Expend.	Current Expend.	National Income	1+2	1 as % of 4	1 as % of 3
	1	2	3	4	5	6
1951	3·1	30·8	186·0	33·9	9·1	1·6
1952	7·8	44·4	217·0	52·2	14·9	3·6
1953	12·3	50·1	244·0	62·4	19·7	5·0
1954	20·9	53·7	248·0	74·6	28·0	8·9
1955	32·0	55·2	289·3	87·2	36·7	10·6
1956	43·0	70·2	334·8	113·2	37·9	12·8
1957	57·4	73·8	352·7	131·2	43·7	16·2
1958	52·4	79·2	374·0	131·6	39·8	14·0
1959	49·9	100·1	391·6	150·0	33·2	12·7
1960	47·5	114·2	437·1	161·7	29·3	10·8
1961	60·8	119·1	484·2	179·9	33·7	12·5
1962	58·7	128·4	528·0	187·1	31·4	11·1
1963	53·5	149·0	525·0	202·5	26·4	10·2
1964	74·0	176·9	595·0	250·9	29·5	12·4
1965	57·1	172·2	632·0	229·3	24·9	9·0
1951–58	228·7	457·8	2,281·8	686·5	33·3	10·0
1959–65	401·5	995·9	3,529·9	1,397·4	28·7	11·4
1951–65	630·2	1,417·7	5,874·7	2,047·9	30·7	10·7

Source: Table IV.1; Central Bank of Iraq, *Quarterly Bulletin*, No. 59, p. 42; Bulletin, *New Series, No, 3*, 1967, p. 26 and No. 4, 1967, p. 24; *Annual Report*, 1963, p. 150; Fenelon, *Iraq, National Income and Expenditure and International Financial Statistics*, Vol. XXI, No. 6, June 1968, p. 176

Note: National income figures are for calendar years while other figures are for financial years

increased from I.D. 25.9 million to I.D. 48.7 million between 1960 and 1965 but expenditure on defence and security increased from I.D. 44.0 million to I.D. 74.6 million during the same period.

The movements of current and capital expenditure during the two periods are shown in Table IV.8. During the first period 1951–58 capital expenditure increased more rapidly than ordinary expenditure and the ratio of capital expenditure to total capital and current expenditure rose from 9.2% in 1951 to 40% in 1958. During the second period the ratio declined sharply to 25% in 1965. Column (6) of Table IV.8 shows that on average capital expenditure by the Development Board and the Planning Board came to almost 11% of national income, at current prices, during 1951–65. The ratio was higher during the second period but this is due to the inclusion of the first year (1951), which was a preliminary year. What is more important than the overall ratio is the trend; thus the ratio started to rise from the low level of 1.6% in 1951 and reached the high level of 16% in 1957. But it was declining during 1959–65 and by 1965 it had reached a low level of 9%.

The rapid expansion of current expenditure, most of which went to security and defence, the decline in the share of oil revenues devoted to capital formation, and the decline in capital expenditure as a percentage of total expenditure and national income, were all movements in the wrong direction from the point of view of economic growth. Nevertheless, the amount of current expenditure on the planning administration increased moderately during 1959–65, while capital expenditure remained stagnant or even declined slightly. But implementation does not depend on the size of the administration alone, and the decline in the capacity of the administration to implement the plans may be partly explained by the fact that the planning organization and administration were made more complicated after the reorganization of 1959. There was no clear distribution of functions or delegation of responsibilities to ministers and departments and the whole process of planning and implementation tended to be slower after the abolition of the Development Board organization.[9]

The result of faulty organization and weak administration was, not surprisingly, increased underspending. The underspending was higher in the industrial sector as can be seen from Table IV.2. This reflects the relatively greater weakness of the administration which dealt with the industrial sector, for although the country has been developing administrative and technical machinery for plan formulation and implementation for a long time, the weakness and inadequate staffing of the machinery in view of the task assigned to it had not been overcome.[10] As a result, most of the

74 ROLE OF GOVERNMENT IN INDUSTRIALIZATION OF IRAQ

industrial projects in the plans were not fully studied, from either a technical or economic point of view. For example, at the beginning of 1965, out of 39 major industrial manufacturing projects included in the 1961–65 plan—all of which were also in the 1959–60 plan—only four projects were completed. Six were under construction, the feasibility of ten was still being studied, and the feasibility studies of nine had been completed.[11] For those nine, the technical engineering specifications had still to be prepared, after that bids for construction would have to be invited and a contractor or contractors chosen before actual construction could start. At all these stages a project had to go through the cumbersome procedure outlined in Chapter II.

TABLE IV.9

Main Elements of Government Ordinary Budget Expenditure, 1951–65

I.D. Millions

Year	Total	Security and Defence	Health and Educatn.	Planning Admin.	4 as % of 1	2 as % of 1	3 as % of 1
	1	2	3	4	5	6	7
1951	30·9	10·9	6·6	0·9	2·9	35·2	21·3
1952	44·7	17·0	8·2	1·2	2·7	38·0	18·3
1953	50·5	18·6	9·2	1·7	3·4	36·8	18·2
1954	54·1	20·1	11·1	2·0	3·7	37·1	20·5
1955	55·7	22·2	12·0	2·1	3·8	39·8	21·5
1956	70·9	28·6	14·6	4·0	5·6	40·3	20·5
1957	74·5	30·6	15·5	2·2	2·9	41·1	20·8
1958	79·9	31·2	17·2	2·9	3·6	39·0	21·5
1959	100·5	37·3	21·5	1·7	1·7	37·1	21·3
1960	114·3	44·1	25·9	3·2	2·8	38·6	22·6
1961	119·2	45·1	30·2	3·5	2·9	37·8	25·3
1962	128·4	49·3	34·2	3·6	2·8	38·4	26·6
1963	149·0	61·3	34·4	3·6	2·4	41·1	23·0
1964	141·7	56·8	34·5	n.a.	n.a.	40·1	24·3
1965	172·2	74·6	48·7	n.a.	n.a.	43·3	28·2
1951–58	461·2			17·0	3·7		
1959–63	611·4			15·7	2·6		

Source: Ministry of Finance, Department of Accounts, *Annual Reports* for the years 1959 through 1963. Central Bank of Iraq, *Quarterly Bulletin*, No. 59, p. 44 and *Bulletin, New Series*, Nos. 3 and 4, 1967, pp. 26 and 24

Notes: (1) n.a. = not available
(2) Column 4 is total administrative expenditure of the Development Board and Ministries and Departments of Industry, Agriculture, Planning, Communication and Buildings
(3) The figures for 1951–58 of Column 3 have been adjusted to include expenditure on primary education to make them comparable with 1959–65 figures

The relatively greater weakness of the organization dealing with

IMPLEMENTATION OF GOVT. INVESTMENT PROGRAMMES 75

industry was partly due to the reorganization of the planning machinery in 1959. Before that time the Development Board gave a low priority to industry and invested little in this sector, and therefore created only a small administration to deal with it. Moreover, outside the Board's organization there were other Government departments dealing with agriculture, communication and public buildings which had been engaged in the implementation of projects almost since the establishment of Iraqi Government in 1921. No similar department dealt with industrialization.

When the functions of the Development Board were divided among different ministries in the manner discussed in Chapter II, a small Ministry of Industry emerged with only a few staff. Although the Planning Board gave first priority in the fifth and sixth plans to industry, the administrative machinery dealing with this sector was not enlarged sufficiently, mainly because administration came under the control of the Ministry of Finance and not the Planning Board. This lack of co-ordination between the plans and the budget (i.e. development policy and fiscal policy) was a real problem and was not reduced by making the Minister of Finance a member of the Planning Board. To show the lack of co-ordination between plans and budgets a comparison is made in Table IV.10 between the public buildings sector and the industrial sector. Columns (1) and (2) of this table show that in 1959 the administrative expenditures of the departments dealing with the implementation of building projects were almost six times the administrative expenditure of departments dealing with the implementation of industrial projects. Columns (3) and (4) of the same table show that during the same year actual capital expenditure on buildings was almost five times the capital expenditure on industrial projects. During that year planned investment in building was three times that of industry. By 1963 while planned expenditure in industry was raised to 120% of planned investment in buildings, administrative expenditure on industry was only 27% of that on buildings. Consequently, underspending in the industrial sector was much higher than in the public buildings sector and capital expenditure in industry came to only 44% of that in the buildings sector.

There is a relationship between administrative expenditure and capital expenditure in each sector. Column (10) of Table IV.10 shows that during the period 1959–63, administrative expenditure represented on average 1.9% of capital expenditure in the industrial sector. Other things being equal, in order to spend I.D. 39.6 million in the industrial sectors in 1963 (which was the planned investment in that sector at that time), one would expect administrative expenditure on industry to be I.D. 752,000. But during that year actual

TABLE IV.10

Administrative Expenditure, Planned Investment and Actual Capital Expenditure in the Building Sector and the Industrial Sector, 1959–63

I.D. Thousands

Year	Administrative Expenditure		Capital Expenditure		Planned Capital Expenditure		2 as % of 1	6 as % of 5	4 as % of 3	2 as % of 4
	Buildings	Industry	Buildings	Industry	Buildings	Industry				
	1	*2*	*3*	*4*	*5*	*6*	*7*	*8*	*9*	*10*
1959	428	72	22,200	4,800	29,800	9,400	16·8	31·5	21·6	1·5
1960	445	132	23,100	5,600	70,000	12,500	29·7	17·8	24·2	2·3
1961	491	160	35,900	7,100	38,100	14,200	32·5	37·2	19·7	2·2
1962	605	168	26,900	10,300	30,700	24,600	27·8	80·1	38·3	1·6
1963	505	187	21,300	9,500	32,900	39,600	37·0	120·4	44·6	2·0
1959–63		719		37,300						1·9

Source: Compiled from Annual Reports of the Department of Accounts, Ministry of Finance for the years 1959 to 1963 and Tables IV.3 and IV.4

Note: Administration Expenditure on Industry is total expenditure of the Departments of Planning, Design and Construction and Industrial Buildings of the Ministry of Industry, while administrative expenditure on buildings are those of the Departments of Building and Housing of the Ministry of Public Buildings and Housing

administrative expenditure on this sector was only I.D. 187,000, i.e., one quarter of the required amount. In fact during that year actual capital expenditure was only slightly more than one quarter of the planned investment in the industrial sector.

No doubt other factors beside administrative expenditures also contribute to the implementation capacity of operating ministries. For example, the internal organization of each ministry, the quality of its staff, and the relative complexity of the field of work are all relevant, but our analysis indicates that administrative expenditure is very important. So far as administrative expenditure determined the capacity of ministries to implement projects, however, Table IV.10 shows that the priorities of the Planning Board were apparently ignored. Other policy makers, mainly the Ministry of Finance, decided the desirable expansion of the capacity of operating ministries or implementing machinery. Such a problem is less likely to occur under the Development Board type of organization, in which plan formulation is not isolated from plan implementation. Implementation machinery was also under the control of the Board and it could change the implementation capacity of departments dealing with different sectors without any need for approval from the Ministry of Finance.

This problem is presumably one of the reasons that led the Minister of Planning to demand, in his introductory statement to Law No. 70 of 1961 for the Five-Year Plan 1961–65, that the Planning Board—and hence its technical secretariat, the Ministry of Planning—must 'participate' in the preparation of the government's annual ordinary budget. The Ministry of Finance apparently did not agree with this view,[12] but Law No. 44 of 1964 dealing with the Planning Board made the 'supervision' of the preparation of the ordinary budget one of the tasks of the Planning Board. This law seems to have had no administrative effect, and Law No. 87 of 1965 for the 1965–69 plan again stressed the importance of 'participation' by the Board in the preparation of the ordinary budget. A later law, No. 18 of 1966, reduced the role of the Planning Board to 'an expression of opinion', which is not only less effective than 'participation' but even less effective than the supervisory role mentioned in the earlier law.

The failure of the Planning Board to obtain adequate staff for the Ministry of Industry, or alternatively the insistence of the Board on formulating plans that bore no relationship to the implementing capacity of the Ministry of Industry, goes a long way to explain the inability of the Ministry to implement industrial projects in sufficiently large numbers to fulfil the industrial investment targets set out by the Board.

78 ROLE OF GOVERNMENT IN INDUSTRIALIZATION OF IRAQ

The institutional set-up was such that planners could not do much about the capacity of operating ministries to implement projects. But the Board could have rendered a great service by preparing plans which took account of the capacity of the administration to implement, instead of ignoring this capacity, and which also recognized that the Government's political will to develop was measured by the 50% of oil revenues it made available, instead of over-estimating this will and expecting plan revenues to be twice the 50% of expected oil revenues. Plan targets would have been much smaller than those of the actual plans which after all were never realized—but planners could have demonstrated that little could be achieved because of lack of a sufficient political will to develop and because of administrative inadequacy. This might have persuaded the Government to do something better.

Political Instability: A United Nations study in 1966 pointed out that political instability was an important factor in explaining poor implementation of plans in Iraq, because 'political instability has weakened decision-making by the various government authorities'.[13] Although no one who is familiar with recent developments in Iraq finds this surprising, it is nevertheless not easy to analyse its significance. However, I have shown in Chapter III that most of the industrial projects included in the later plans originated in the Little report.[14] Most of these projects were included in the 1955–60 plan of the Development Board and were studied or were under study before the 1958 Revolution when a number of western consulting engineering and contracting firms were dismissed and their places taken by Soviet experts. Further studies and preparation of feasibility studies, technical specifications, etc., by Soviet experts was of course time consuming. For example one industrial project (sulphur extraction from natural gas) went through the whole process of pre-construction before 1958, and in June of that year the Development Board decided to contract the erection of the plant to an American firm at a total cost of I.D. 6,680,320. The firm was asked to approach the Ministry of Development to sign the required agreement. Then the Revolution of July 1958 intervened and the firm was informed that the new Government had decided to abrogate the Board's decision. The project was included in the Iraqi-Soviet Technical and Economic Co-operation Agreement of May 1959, to be studied and designed during 1959–62 and erected during 1962–64. After the Revolution of February 1963, the project was withdrawn from the agreement and the process of reviewing and restudying started again. By January 1965 the contract for the erection of the project was signed with the original American firm at a cost of I.D. 7,485,900 for exactly the old

IMPLEMENTATION OF GOVT. INVESTMENT PROGRAMMES 79

project. Thus not only were seven years wasted during which income from the project was lost, but the cost of the projects also increased substantially.

This example shows the harmful effect of political instability. More generally Table IV.1 shows that capital expenditure started to rise slowly in the early 1950s, but the process was accelerating, and capital expenditure increased from I.D. 3.1 million in 1951 to I.D. 57.4 million in 1957. The momentum was then lost for many years after the 1958 Revolution; eventually expenditure started to rise again but was interrupted by another Revolution in 1963 and capital expenditures decreased again.

REFERENCES

1. Waterson, *Development Planning*, p. 299
2. Reddaway, *Importance of Time Lag for Economic Planning*, p. 227
3. See Table I.6, p. 11 and Central Bank of Iraq, *Annual Report*, 1965, p. 18
4. Ministry of Finance, Department of Accounts, *Annual Report*, 1959, p. 10
5. See Table III.10, p. 47
6. See pp. 50–52
7. Tinbergen, *Central Planning*, p. 72
8. Figures for the other two years, 1964–65, were not yet published by the Department of Accounts of the Ministry of Finance
9. See p. 25
10. United Nations, *Industrial Programming and Policies in Selected Countries of the Middle East*, p. 45
11. *Ibid.*, p. 43
12. Ministry of Guidance, *The Five Year Plan 1961–65*, p. 63
13. United Nations, *Industrial Planning and Policies in Selected Countries of the Middle East*, p. 45
14. See p. 39

Chapter V

FINANCIAL INSTITUTIONS AND INDUSTRIALIZATION
1950–65

The purpose of this chapter is to examine Government policy towards institutions concerned with the finance of private industry. By far the most important of these institutions was the Industrial Bank created in 1946 and fully owned by the Government. A detailed analysis of the role of this bank forms the main subject of this chapter, but I will also consider the past and potential roles of the Central Bank and commercial banks. The Central Bank was established in 1947 by the Government to control monetary policy. The Government also created in 1942 one of the largest commercial banks of Iraq, namely the Rafidain Bank, and it nationalized all commercial banks in 1964. All these institutions were attached to regular ministries. The central Government was legally in charge of monetary policy and could control it.

1. *Commercial Banks and the Finance of Industry*

In discussions of underdeveloped countries an important place is usually given to the shortage of capital both in the sense of real physical assets and of funds to finance their construction. The latter has two aspects: the necessary saving, and the purely financial aspect of channelling savings towards specific objectives. My analysis will be confined to the financial mechanism only.

Industrial expansion requires investment funds which come either from within the enterprises themselves (internal finance) or from external sources, namely banks and the capital market. The most important sources of external finance are loans and capital funds provided in exchange for shares. Loans can be classified according to their terms of maturity into short, intermediate and long terms, that is for periods of less than one year, one to ten years and more than ten years. Short term loans are granted by commercial banks and are usually intended for the finance of working capital while longer term loans are intended to finance fixed capital formation.

In underdeveloped countries planners and private entrepreneurs tend to concentrate on the finance required for fixed capital forma-

FINANCIAL INSTITUTIONS AND INDUSTRIALIZATION 81

tion and devote limited attention to the equally important working capital requirements. For example the 1965–69 Iraqi plan allocated only I.D. 5 million for working capital and provided I.D. 141 million for fixed investment in the manufacturing industry.[1] Furthermore, most writing on problems of industrialization does not treat adequately the need for working capital. Yet many industrial enterprises may fail because firms are unable to obtain the necessary working capital from banks. It is evident that an adequate assessment of the volume of working capital is required and ways and means of financing it are necessary if financial bottlenecks are to be avoided.

The main components of working capital include: inventories, receivables and cash at hand or in banks. Working capital requirements differ from enterprise to enterprise, and depend on capital intensity, seasonality, location, business practices, etc. Differences tend to be small between enterprises in the same branch of industry but widen between industrial sectors. Table V.1 shows relative working capital requirements for thirty major industrial enterprises in Iraq. It is interesting to notice that in two companies producing vegetable oil the ratio of the value of current assets to the value of fixed assets had the same magnitude (124), the two spinning and weaving companies have also the same ratio (82), the ratio for the four cement enterprises was between 29 and 44. This shows that the ratio was far lower in the capital intensive industry—cement— than in the textile industry—which one expects to be less capital intensive. The ratio was also relatively low for a number of industries such as matches, jute and nylon stockings, which imported their raw materials throughout the year, while it was higher for cigarette manufacturing companies, which usually in Iraq buy most of the tobacco they need for the whole year at the end of the tobacco season. The shorter the time for which raw materials have to be held, the less funds are required on balance in working capital. The table also reveals that in most enterprises, working capital was larger than fixed capital. This demonstrates the importance of working capital, a large part of which can be financed by short term loans from commercial banks.

A breakdown of commercial loans by sectors is, unfortunately, not available. The law for the control of banking authorized the Central Bank to require banks to supply it with annual and monthly balance sheets in a prescribed form.[2] Commercial banks were not, however, required to submit breakdowns of their loans by sectors, nor did they keep such statistics for their own information,[3] but partial evidence is available which indicates the smallness of commercial banks' loans to the industrial sector. Table V.2 shows the

82 ROLE OF GOVERNMENT IN INDUSTRIALIZATION OF IRAQ

TABLE V.1

The Ratio of Working Capital to Fixed Capital in Thirty Major Industrial Companies in Iraq in 1962

Name	Product	Ratio of Working to Fund Capital
National Leather Industries	Leather	210
Iraq Carpet Company	Carpets	133
Cotton Seed Products Company	Vegetable Oil	124
Vegetable Oil Extraction Company	Vegetable Oil	124
Al-Ahliya Tobacco Company	Cigarettes	102
Rafidain Tobacco Company	Cigarettes	93
Iraq Detergent Company	Detergent	87
Asbestos Industries Co.	Asbestos	86
Iraq Spinning and Weaving Company	Textiles	82
Fattah Pasha Spinning and Weaving Co.	Textiles	82
Northern Industries Company	Beverages	76
Eastern Industries Company	Beverages	64
Euphrates Industries Company	Beverages	62
Arab Carbonated Water Company	Beverages	57
Eastern Beer Company	Beverages	55
Shatt El-Arab Industries	Beverages	50
National Cardboard Company	Cardboard	68
Iraq Jute Industries Company	Jute Products	59
United Match Factory	Matches	58
Agrarian Industries Company	Food Products	57
Nylon Stocking Company	Stockings	57
Kerbala Cotton Textile Company	Cotton Textile	56
Northern Grain Milling Company	Flour	55
Dates Industries Company	Dates	45
Rafidain Cement Company	Cement	44
Iraq Cement Company	Cement	41
Euphrates Cement Company	Cement	37
United Cement Company	Cement	29
Iraqi Building Material Company	Building Materials	35
Eastern Chemical Industries	Gas	26
Total (30 Companies)		**64**

Source: U.N. *Financing of Manufacturing Industry*, p. A.15

consolidated balance sheet of 30 major industrial companies in 1962. It shows that the combined indebtedness of these companies to the commercial banks amounted to only I.D. 1 million, or 4% of their total liabilities.

In terms of paid up capital these companies accounted for about one third of private industry at that time.[4] If we assume that the indebtedness of these enterprises to the commercial banks could be regarded as representative of the private industrial sector as a whole, then the total indebtedness of the private industrial sector to the commercial banks would be I.D. 3 million.

In 1962, however, total claims of the commercial banks on the private sector were I.D. 62 million.[5] This means that the propor-

FINANCIAL INSTITUTIONS AND INDUSTRIALIZATION 83

tion of outstanding private industrial short term credit to total claims of commercial banks on the private sector would have been 5%. But because these thirty companies were well established it can be argued that the indebtedness of the rest of the private industrial sector to banks was probably less.

TABLE V.2

Consolidated Balance Sheet of Thirty Major Industrial Companies 1962–63

I.D. Thousands

Liabilities	Amount	%
Net worth:	22,055	81
Paid-up Capital	17,212	64
Undistributed Profits	2,477	9
Capital Reserves	2,366	9
Medium- and Long-term Loans:	855	3
Industrial Bank	551	2
Other	304	1
Current Debt:	4,238	16
Short term bank credits	1,029	4
Creditors	2,023	8
Income tax reserves	884	3
Other	297	1
Owner's equity and total liabilities	27,148	100

Assets	Amount	%
Gross fixed assets	20,894	77
Minus: reserves for depreciation	10,107	37
Net fixed assets	10,787	40
Intangible assets	3,048	11
Current assets	13,314	49
Cash in hand and at banks	1,404	5
Inventories	8,879	33
Debtors	2,803	10
Other	194	1
Total assets	27,148	100

Source: United Nations, *Financing of Manufacturing Industry*, p. A.14

Such a meagre extension of bank credit to the industrial sector can hardly be explained by lack of demand. Thus Table V.2 shows that the same thirty industrial enterprises were obliged to resort to another source of short term credit, namely, suppliers' credit, and the volume of this type of credit was twice as large as the volume of bank credit. Both types of funds accomplish the same purpose in meeting operating expenses, thus an enterprise may finance part of its working capital directly by means of trade credit or indirectly by cash borrowing, which is later used for making inventory purchases. But trade credit is usually more expensive than bank credit.

84 ROLE OF GOVERNMENT IN INDUSTRIALIZATION OF IRAQ

For example even in the United Kingdom the rate of interest on such credit is $2\frac{1}{2}\%$ for one month.[6] If we assume that the rate was even as low as 1% a month in Iraq, the effective rate of interest charged will be 12% per annum compared with a rate of interest of only 7% charged by Iraq's commercial banks.[7]

It is evident that industrialists will not resort to such an expensive form of credit if they can borrow from banks. But such extensive dependence by industrialists on suppliers' credit is a familiar sign of 'credit hunger'. Moreover, in 1961 the Industrial Bank decided to resume activities in the field of short-term lending, in order, among other things, to ease shortage in the supply of short-term credit.[8] Earlier the situation was apparently no better, and in 1956 the consultants to the Development Board, Arthur D. Little, noticed that private industrial enterprises 'including those established by the Industrial Bank, find serious difficulties in obtaining adequate supplies of working capital'.[9] The question is, why did the commercial banks fail to meet the demands of industry for credit? Was it because of an absence of liquidity? Were deposits in banks highly volatile and hence banks needed high reserve ratios? Did the Central Bank try to encourage commercial banks to lend more to industry?

Table V.3, shows that during the period 1950–58 commercial banks maintained a cash reserve ratio against their private deposit liabilities (item 10) considerably higher than the 15% imposed by the Central Bank.[10] This ratio varied between a low level of 26% in 1956 and a high level of 48% in 1950. Although the ratio fell sharply during 1959–65 it remained well above the legal ratio imposed by the Central Bank. During 1950–65 the cash reserve ratio against total deposit liabilities (item 11) was also high. Throughout the same period commercial banks maintained substantial amounts of excess reserves, defined as the difference between legally required reserves and total reserves.

During the first period 1950–58 they were highly liquid and the liquidity ratio[11]—defined as the ratio of total liquid assets (including cash in hand, deposits at Central Bank, Treasury Bills, gold and short-term foreign assets and commercial bills rediscountable at the Central Bank) against liabilities, varied between 70% at the end of 1952 and 46% at the end of 1956. After 1958 the ratio fell from 53% to 36% at the end of 1965. Yet commercial banks still remained highly liquid and maintained large amounts of excess reserves. Thus the lack of liquidity cannot explain the failure of commercial banks to supply industry with sufficient amounts of short-term credit.

Table V.3 shows that in early 1950 there was a marked preference

TABLE V.3

Consolidated Balance Sheet, Liquidity Ratios and Excess Reserves of Iraqi Commercial Banks, 1950–65

I.D. Millions

	1950	1951	1952	1953	1954	1955	1956	1957	1958	1959	1960	1961	1962	1963	1964	1965
Assets																
1 Reserves	9·7	7·8	9·5	12·2	10·4	11·4	10·0	12·9	17·8	14·7	15·6	12·2	11·8	13·7	14·9	17·3
Currency	4·6	5·0	4·1	4·2	4·9	4·9	5·2	3·9	4·1	5·8	6·1	3·7	3·9	5·1	4·7	4·1
At Central Bank	5·0	2·8	5·4	7·9	5·5	6·5	4·7	9·0	13·6	8·9	9·5	8·5	7·8	8·6	10·2	13·2
2 Foreign Assets	10·3	13·7	19·0	21·3	23·7	21·8	12·7	20·6	24·4	23·9	16·1	12·3	12·0	12·9	8·9	10·0
3 Claims on Government	3·6	3·8	2·3	2·0	2·4	3·0	2·7	2·2	2·3	9·3	10·4	6·7	7·6	4·6	7·6	20·6
4 Claims on Private Sector	6·0	11·3	16·8	15·5	24·8	31·1	32·8	38·8	38·0	42·8	51·3	59·8	62·2	64·3	67·8	61·8
Liabilities																
5 Demand Deposits	12·8	13·3	13·4	16·6	19·4	21·3	24·5	28·7	31·8	30·9	29·6	29·1	33·1	30·0	29·0	30·4
6 Quasi-Monetary Liabilities	7·2	9·4	8·6	9·3	10·0	11·7	14·7	17·4	20·3	24·9	28·8	33·1	34·9	36·9	38·4	45·2
7 Government Deposits	6·2	10·5	15·6	19·9	25·0	26·0	8·2	11·0	16·6	20·6	16·7	13·6	11·5	12·1	13·8	17·2
8 Foreign Liabilities	—	0·3	0·1	0·1	1·7	1·1	1·2	1·1	0·7	0·5	0·8	1·0	1·0	0·9	0·7	0·9
9 Capital Accounts	3·2	2·7	3·1	4·6	5·6	7·2	8·8	10·4	11·5	11·5	11·8	13·1	14·8	15·8	16·1	15·7
10 Cash Reserve Ratio 1÷(5+6)(100)	48	34	43	47	35	35	26	28	34	26	27	20	17	20	22	23
11 Cash Reserve Ratio: 1÷(5+6+7)(100)	37	24	25	27	19	19	21	23	26	19	21	16	15	17	18	19
12 Foreign Assets Ratio: 2÷(5+6+7)(100)	39	41	50	46	43	37	27	36	35	31	21	16	15	16	10	10
13 Local Earning Assets Ratio: (3+4)100−(5+6+7)	36	42	35	38	50	57	75	70	58	68	82	87	87	86	90	67
14 Excess Reserves	8·4	6·0	7·5	9·8	7·4	5·8	6·2	8·1	12·1	9·5	10·3	6·6	5·4	7·6	7·8	8·5
15 Liquidity Ratio	48	34	43	47	35	35	26	27	34	26	27	20	17	21	22	23

Source: Central Bank of Iraq, *Bulletin, New Series*, No. 1, 1965, pp. 16–17 and No. 4, 1967, pp. 12–13

Notes: (1) Excess Reserves and liquidity ratio are defined on page 84
     (2) Unclassified assets and liabilities have been excluded

86 ROLE OF GOVERNMENT IN INDUSTRIALIZATION OF IRAQ

for foreign assets, thus the ratio of foreign assets to total deposits maintained by commercial banks was as high as 50% at the end of 1952, but fell thereafter to reach 10.7% at the end of 1965. Item 13 of the table shows the opposite trend for local assets to liability ratio which increased from the low level of 36% at the end of 1950 to 88% at the end of 1965. Thus one cannot explain the smallness of credit extended to industry by arguing that bankers preferred foreign assets. The fact is that bankers preferred other local assets to local industrial assets.

Although there was a considerable increase in the claims of the commercial banks on the private sector (item 4), the banks nevertheless, followed a conservative policy, especially towards the industrial sector. Commercial banks of Iraq were liquid enough to have supplied industry with a considerable amount of short term credit had they been willing to do so.

A central bank could have encouraged commercial banks to provide industry with more credit. In fact the Central Bank was established by the Government in 1947 and made responsible for monetary and credit policy and among its explicitly stated functions was to facilitate the provision of credit for trade, industry and agri culture.[12] In 1950 the Bank was given the traditional powers of central banks to control commercial banks by operating on the bank rate, changing the legal reserve requirements of commercial banks, controlling the ratio of commercial banks' total deposits that could be invested abroad and undertaking open market operations in unspecified assets.[13] But under Law No. 72 of 1956 open market operations were confined to Government securities and paper eligible for rediscount. The latter was limited to treasury bills and inland bills of exchange or promissory notes arising out of commercial transactions maturing within three months.

Yet the Central Bank has played a very small role. It had no control over specialized banks, such as the Industrial Bank, and its control over the commercial banks was formal and very weak at its best. 'The Bank was no more than an agency engaged in transferring foreign exchange into Iraqi currency'.[14] Its loans to commercial banks were negligible; its total loans and advances to these banks at the end of 1965 were only I.D. 2.1 million[15] compared with the total local assets of the commercial banks of more than I.D. 80 million[16] at the same time. The reason was that commercial banks did not require credit because they were already highly liquid. Nevertheless, the Central Bank might well have encouraged commercial banks to provide industry with more working capital. It might have induced them to ease their lending policy through the provision of generous discount facilities either in the form of

FINANCIAL INSTITUTIONS AND INDUSTRIALIZATION 87

lower interest rates or longer term loans on paper arising out of loans to the industrial sector. The Bank could have adopted even more specific measures so that credit extended to certain sectors should not exceed a fixed amount, or a given proportion of the total credit supply. While it is not certain that a more active policy by the Bank would have met with much success it did not even try.

Iraq's commercial banks could have expanded their short term loans to industry. An interesting question is whether they could have financed fixed capital. Table V.4 shows that private deposits on demand with commercial banks amounted to I.D. 13.4 million while time and saving deposits amounted to I.D. 2.3 million, at the end of 1952; by the end of 1963 the latter amounted to I.D. 30 million while demand deposits increased to I.D. 29.5 million. By the end of 1965 time and saving deposits had risen to I.D. 36 million —six millions more than demand deposits. Column 6 of the table shows that the velocity of time and saving deposits was not only low but declined in later years. Commercial banks might be venturesome if demand deposits also displayed a very low rate of turnover, but this was not the case in Iraq. In fact the velocity of circula-

TABLE V.4

Volume, Withdrawals and Velocity of Circulation of Demand, Time and Saving Deposits of the Private Sector with Iraq's Commercial Banks 1952–65

I.D. Millions

Year	Demand Deposits	Time and Saving Deposits	Withdrawals from Demand Deposits	Withdrawals from Time Deposits	Velocity of Demand Deposits	Velocity of Saving Deposits
	1	*2*	*3*	*4*	*5*	*6*
1952	13·4	2·3	221	3·0	16·4	1·3
1953	16·6	3·3	257	2·5	15·4	0·7
1954	19·4	4·3	325	4·3	16·7	1·0
1955	21·3	5·7	416	7·1	19·5	1·2
1956	24·5	7·8	464	8·3	18·9	1·06
1957	28·7	12·7	559	12·7	19·4	1·0
1958	31·8	15·7	561	20·4	17·6	1·2
1959	30·9	17·5	516	20·5	16·6	1·17
1960	30·2	21·2	579	18·3	19·1	0·86
1961	29·5	24·4	622	19·6	21·0	0·8
1962	33·5	28·4	744	22·0	22·2	0·77
1963	30·5	29·0	705	27·3	23·1	0·9
1964	29·5	30·1	758	30·3	25·1	1·0
1965	31·0	36·0	782	37·0	25·2	1·0

Source: Central Bank of Iraq, *Bulletin, New Series*, No. 4, 1967, pp. 12, 20

88 ROLE OF GOVERNMENT IN INDUSTRIALIZATION OF IRAQ

tion of private demand deposits with commercial banks was high in 1952 and increased after that. During later years these deposits were used almost twice per month compared with once every two and a half months in Lebanon during 1964.[17] Nevertheless, due to the large and increasing percentage of time and saving deposits in total deposits and because of the regularity in velocity, one can say that deposits in Iraq were not volatile and could have been used not only for short term lending but for some longer term loans as well.

Traditionally commercial banks have displayed a strong bias against long term loans. Bankers usually argue that since their liabilities are withdrawable on demand or at short notice, their assets must also be short term, because if they invest a significant part of their deposits in long term claims which cannot be liquidated easily any nervousness on the part of depositors might cause a financial crisis.

No doubt there is a core of truth to this argument. Nevertheless, both Sayers and Nevin hold that commercial banks should give more medium and long term credit.[18] A commercial banker is able to make profits because he knows that repayment of his deposits is not required in total at any one time, and a substantial part of deposits may not be demanded permanently, thus opening up a source of long term finance. Conservative banking practice would, however, reject the possibility of using funds acquired on a short term basis to grant longer term credit, and would confine portfolios to short term self-liquidating paper to avoid the danger of illiquidity. But in times of crisis this danger involves not only long term assets but also short term claims if adequate rediscounting facilities are not available. Consequently, if it is desirable to use any significant part of the funds of commercial banks acquired on a short term basis for the purchase of long term claims, provision of rediscounting facilities for claims arising from long term industrial finance is essential.

The Central Bank of Iraq discouraged commercial banks from granting long term credit by confining its discount facilities to short term bills of exchange or promissory notes of three months' maturity. It did nothing whatsoever to encourage commercial banks to extend all types of credit to the industrial sector. Presumably it left all types of industrial finance to the Industrial Bank to take care of. The Central Bank did not bother to inquire into the needs of industry for finance and it had no credit policy in this respect.

2. *The Industrial Bank*

The Agricultural-Industrial Bank started operation in 1936 to meet the short and long term credit needs of agriculture and

FINANCIAL INSTITUTIONS AND INDUSTRIALIZATION 89

industry.[19] Throughout the first decade of its operation the Bank was more interested in agriculture than in industry and from 1936 to 1945 the annual loans granted to agriculture averaged I.D. 75,500 compared with only I.D. 6,300 for industry. At the end of the financial year 1945 the outstanding participation of the Bank in the equity of industrial enterprises amounted to only I.D. 118,000,[20] which is insignificant.

In order to devote more attention to industry and secure specialization in the operation of the Bank, the Government decided in 1940 to separate the Bank into an Industrial Bank and an Agricultural Bank.[21] Because of the war the separation did not take place until 1946, when the Industrial Bank started operations.

The purpose of the Bank was to encourage the industrialization of Iraq. To achieve this aim it was permitted to make loans to industrial enterprises, participate in the equity capital of industrial companies, facilitate the import of machinery and raw materials for industrial purposes, establish and operate warehouses, engage in ordinary banking operations, deal with foreign exchange, issue guarantees and provide technical assistance and advice on administrative, engineering and accounting affairs as well as preparation of feasibility studies.[22] Thus legally the Bank was far more than a credit institution, and in this section I intend to evaluate the operations of the Bank over the period 1950–65 in the light of its established functions.

Resources of the Bank

To operate properly the Bank would have to have sufficient financial resources. Up to 1950 it was handicapped by a shortage of capital at its disposal. According to the 1940 Law its nominal capital was set at I.D. 500,000, but with the sharp increase in prices during the war the purchasing power of the Iraqi dinar during the post-war period, was about a quarter of the 1940 level. Moreover, as the capital of the Bank was provided by a Government loan 'the Treasury decided what amounts to pay and when to pay them and its decisions often did not coincide with the Bank's requests either for funds or for making forward plans'.[23] The situation changed in early 1950, and the capital of the Bank was increased to one million dinars.

Table V.5 shows that, during the period 1950–58, paid-up capital was increased from one million dinar to I.D. 3.7 million; every time the Bank used up its resources additional resources were made available by the Government. But during 1959–65 paid-up capital was increased only once, in 1959, by one million to I.D. 4.7 million. Up to 1963 net profits of the Bank made an important

TABLE V.5

Resources of the Industrial Bank, 1950–65

I.D. Thousands

Year	Nominal Capital	Paid-up Capital	Accumulated Profits	Total Resources
	1	2	3	4
1950	1,000	1,000	73	1,073
1951	1,000	1,000	173	1,173
1952	3,000	2,000	305	2,305
1953	3,000	2,700	329	3,029
1954	3,000	3,000	540	3,540
1955	3,000	3,000	827	3,827
1956	5,000	3,500	993	4,493
1957	8,000	3,750	1,265	5,015
1958	8,000	3,750	1,505	5,255
1959	8,000	4,750	1,640	6,390
1960	8,000	4,750	1,843	6,593
1961	10,000	4,750	2,248	6,998
1962	10,000	4,750	2,383	7,133
1963	10,000	4,750	2,669	7,419
1964	10,000	4,750	2,969	7,719
1965	10,000	4,750	3,061	7,811

Source: The Industrial Bank, *A Report*, March 1965, p. 15 and Ministry of Industry, *The Position of the Industrial Sector in Iraq*, p. 28

contribution to its total resources. But most of these profits came from profits of companies in which the Bank held shares. This can be seen from Table V.6 which shows that during the period 1950–65 61% of its total income came from these profits. In July 1964 most of these companies were nationalized,[24] and the Bank ceased to receive any profits from them. The income of the Bank declined from I.D. 599,321 in 1963 to I.D. 280,200 in 1964.

The moderate amount of profit in 1964 is due to the fact that those companies were nationalized in July of that year but some of them had paid profits to the Bank before that date.[25] During 1965 the Bank did not receive anything from these companies, therefore, its income further declined to I.D. 195,935. Thus since 1960 the Government has not increased the paid-up capital of the Bank and in 1964 an important source of income was eliminated; moreover up to the end of the period under study, the organization responsible for compensating the Bank for its shares in companies that were nationalized has not made any payment to the Industrial Bank.[26] Consequently, the financial position of the Bank has deteriorated in recent years and its capacity to extend loans and participate in industrial enterprises had been seriously restricted. In 1965 the Bank reported that it had practically exhausted all its

FINANCIAL INSTITUTIONS AND INDUSTRIALIZATION

TABLE V.6

Sources of Revenue of the Industrial Bank, 1950–65

I.D. Thousands

Year	Interest	Miscellaneous	Dividends	Total	3 as % of 4
	1	2	3	4	5
1950	20	0	63	83	76
1951	29	0	92	121	76
1956	136	1	129	266	48
1957	132	1	421	554	76
1958	173	1	310	484	64
1959	158	1	232	391	59
1960	166	0	288	454	63
1961	175	2	475	652	70
1962	137	7	182	326	56
1963	180	5	373	558	67
1964	187	4	88	279	31
1965	185	9	1	195	0·5
1956–63					65

Source: The Industrial Bank of Iraq, *Profit and Loss Accounts*, 1950, 1951 and *Annual Reports*, 1956–65

resources and that its activities during that year were based on loan repayments and a loan of I.D. 500,000 from the Central Bank at 3% interest rate per year. The Bank urged the Ministry of Finance and the Planning Board to put at its disposal additional financial resources, but without success.[27]

I have demonstrated in Chapter III that Government policy after 1959 was to industrialize Iraq as rapidly as possible and that the Planning Board devoted large sums of money to investment in the industrial sector,[28] but most of these funds were never utilized and large sums of idle balances were accumulated, as we have shown in Chapter IV.[29] Yet planners failed to appreciate the role of the Industrial Bank in the process of industrialization and did not increase resources available to the Bank despite its persistent demands; instead they formulated plans that ignored the existence of the Industrial Bank.

Long and Medium Term Loans: One of the main functions of the Bank was the extension of medium and long term credit. Table V.7 shows the number and amount of these loans advanced by the Bank since 1950. During that year it granted 93 loans for a total sum of I.D. 131,949. The number of loans increased rapidly until in 1957 nearly 300 loans were granted for a total sum of I.D. 1.5 million. By 1965 although the number of loans increased to 460 the total sum fell to I.D. 0.7 million. The table reveals a rapid decline in the amount of loans granted in recent years mainly as the result

92 ROLE OF GOVERNMENT IN INDUSTRIALIZATION OF IRAQ

of the decreased financial resources of the Bank. Thus in February 1965 the Bank reported that 'if additional financial resources are made available, the Bank will immediately increase all its services to the private sector which in fact needs them. In other words the financial resources at the disposal of the Bank is the limiting factor.'[30]

TABLE V.7

*Number and Amount of Long and Medium Term Loans
Advanced by The Industrial Bank, 1950–65*

Year	Number	I.D.
1950	93	131,949
1951	87	281,224
1952	153	656,949
1953	181	734,140
1954	242	1,367,602
1955	457	735,040
1956	369	745,430
1957	292	1,487,542
1958	237	569,455
1959	388	747,816
1960	389	751,882
1961	472	1,009,402
1962	315	845,941
1963	292	891,040
1964	407	909,903
1965	467	796,323

Source: The Industrial Bank, *A Report*, March 1965, p. 9; The Industrial Bank, *Annual Report*, 1965, p. 22

Table V.8, shows that although most of the Bank's loans were in amounts less than I.D. 1,000, most of its money went to enterprises who borrowed I.D. 5,000 and more. Thus the Bank's policy was apparently biased in favour of medium and large scale enterprises. The Bank's loans have been confined, since 1961, to enterprises which have been licensed by the Ministry of Industry,[31] and required that at least 60% of the capital of the enterprise was owned by Iraqis or Arabs, and that the cost of machinery was not less than I.D. 3,000[32] Thus the Bank excluded from its operations a large number of small enterprises, but since the Bank was the only financial institution granting medium and long term loans, such a policy is hard to justify. Apparently the Bank did not meet demands of small firms because administrative costs of a large number of small loans are usually high, and the risk of default in the smaller firms is usually greater, hence the Bank could make more profits, or less losses, by concentrating on medium and large scale enterprises. The original purpose of the Bank, however, was to encourage industry, not to make profits.

TABLE V.8

Distribution of Loans made by the Industrial Bank According to Size
1961–65

Size of Loan I.D.		1961 Value			1962 Value			1963 Value			1964 Value			1965 Value	
	No.	I.D.	%	No.	I.D.	%	No.	I.D.	%	No.	I.D.	%	No.	I.D.	%
Up to 500	185	61,262	6·07	131	42,294	4·09	102	31,840	3·57	159	50,805	5·58	211	69,400	8·72
5,001–1,000	107	85,408	8·46	42	34,450	4·07	47	41,460	4·65	76	61,201	6·73	79	62,680	7·87
1,001–5,000	139	337,445	37·39	108	265,397	31·37	104	260,640	29·25	135	310,897	34·17	140	342,931	43·06
5,001–10,000	28	215,285	21·33	20	115,800	18·42	19	145,200	16·30	27	216,000	23·74	26	188,712	23·07
Greater than 10,000	13	270,000	26·75	14	348,000	41·14	20	411,900	46·23	10	271,000	29·78	8	132,600	16·65
Total	472	1,009,400	100·00	315	845,941	100·00	292	891,040	100·00	407	909,903	100·00	464	796,323	100·00

Source: Industrial Bank, *Annual Reports*, 1964, p. 16, and, 1965, p. 24

94 ROLE OF GOVERNMENT IN INDUSTRIALIZATION OF IRAQ

The period of a loan could not exceed seven years unless the loan was covered by a mortgage on immovable property, in which case the maximum duration was 12 years.[33] But the Bank's actual policy in this respect was far more conservative. Thus, 'until 1955, well over half of the loans matured in less than three years and very rarely did a term exceed five years'.[34] The annual reports of the Bank during 1958–64 give no information about the length of its loans. Table V.9, shows that during 1965 only 11% of the amount lent was for more than five years. The Bank's loans appear to be for medium terms. This may be in part due to the fact that the industrial sector in Iraq consisted mainly of light industries,[35] which may require quick replacement of capital and rapid amortization. Nevertheless, the short period of loans may partly explain the fact that a rather large proportion of loans were not repaid as they fell due. For example, in 1965 only 30% of matured debts were repaid,[36] hence the Bank was led, in one way or another, to extend the terms of loans, and this could have introduced some confusion into the work of the Bank and use a certain amount of administrative input without having any clear advantage. Moreover, such a high ratio of unrepaid loans may be regarded as a sign that the terms of loans were decided on in a rather haphazard way.

Short-Term Loans: Aside from making medium and long term loans the Bank also extended short term credit for the opening of documentary letters of credit, discounted bills, and extended credit on bonded goods in warehouses.[37] Table V.10 shows the number and value of short term credits extended by the Bank during 1950–65. These short term credits were used to finance imports of machinery, spare parts, as well as raw materials. These short term loans were stopped in 1957 but started again in 1961.[38] Since then the Bank had increased its operation in the field of short term credit normally occupied by commercial banks.

In view of the position of the Industrial Bank in the financial structure of Iraq as the only source of medium and long term industrial credit and because of its limited resources, it was probably unwise for the Bank to compete with commercial banks. Commercial banks did not, however, extend sufficient short term credit to industry. Under these circumstances it perhaps seemed logical for the Industrial Bank to step in. Nevertheless the Bank should have concentrated on the provision of medium and long term credit while the Central Bank should have encouraged commercial banks to provide industry with the short term credit it required. Alternatively, the Industrial Bank might have guaranteed their short term loans to its customers. The point is that commercial banks are less likely to be persuaded to advance long term loans; hence the

FINANCIAL INSTITUTIONS AND INDUSTRIALIZATION

TABLE V.9

Number and Value of Loans by the Industrial Bank According to Maturity, 1965

Term	No.	I.D.	% of Total
One year	54	174,490	21·9
Two years	71	85,330	10·7
Three years	92	65,619	8·3
Four years	60	69,190	8·6
Five years	154	312,692	39·3
More than five years	33	88,552	11·1
Total	464	796,323	100·0

Source: Industrial Bank, *Annual Report*, 1965, p. 26

TABLE V.10

*Value of Short Term Loans Advanced by
The Industrial Bank, 1950–65*

Year	I.D. 000
1950	29
1951	26
1952	57
1953	174
1954	125
1955	438
1956	250
1957	170
1961	113
1962	362
1963	287
1964	441
1965	636

Source: The Industrial Bank, *Annual Reports*, 1950–65

Central Bank should have at least pushed them into the provision of short term credit so that the Industrial Bank could have concentrated on other forms of industrial credit. But neither the Central Bank nor the Industrial Bank seemed to have paid any attention to this problem. In 1965 the latter substantially increased the amount of its short term lending and decreased long term loans, as is clear from Tables V.7 and V.10. This was in part probably the result of lack of direction from the top.

Although the Board of Directors of the Bank made policy within the framework of the law, the responsibility of the Minister of Industry was not limited to the appointment of members of the Board of Directors and the prescribing of the basic status under which the Bank operated. Legally the Minister of Industry could have required the Board to reconsider any decision taken by it.[39] In practice the role of the Minister was reduced to the appointment

96 ROLE OF GOVERNMENT IN INDUSTRIALIZATION OF IRAQ

of members of the Board and a purely routine approval of each single loan extended by the Bank, provided that it was more than I.D. 5,000.[40] This was the result partly of the lack of a research unit inside the Ministry which could follow such developments, and partly of frequent cabinet changes which hardly left time for a Minister to comprehend the complex situation, formulate policy and then supervise its implementation. Thus, during 1959–65, there were eight Ministers of Industry, five of which held office in 1963–65.

The Bank had a free hand in allocating its loans between long term and short term credit. As noted above, the planners and Ministers did not increase the paid up capital of the Bank after 1960, and the Bank came to depend more on interest as a source of income after the nationalization of companies in which it was a shareholder,[41] and in order to make more profits the Bank increased its short term credit, on which it charged 6%[42] per year, and reduced long term loans, for which it charged 4%.[43] In view of the position of the Bank in the financial structure of the economy, this was a very unsatisfactory tendency.

Participation: The Bank's other main function was to help in the promotion of industrial enterprises. Iraqis were, understandably, reluctant to invest in industry[44] and the Bank had to convince potential investors that funds could be safely placed in industry. Before 1961 the Bank could build industrial enterprises directly on its own account,[45] but it preferred to participate with the private sector. The idea was presumably to secure maximum amount of investment in industry with a given amount of public funds, to safeguard against the danger of lack of self-interest in industrial firms, and to attract private entrepreneurial talent into industry.[46] Under the 1961 law the Bank is not allowed to establish industrial enterprises on its own account, but it is allowed to participate with the private sector in the establishment of manufacturing industries.[47]

Up to the end of 1965, the Bank participated in 21 enterprises.[48] Table V.11 shows the participation by the Bank in various companies during 1950–65. The number of enterprises and the amount paid by the Bank increased rapidly before 1958. After that, the process became slower. Moreover, with the exception of the Light Industries Company, all enterprises in which the bank participated after 1958 were small. These are the first six enterprises in Table V.13, which shows that, besides the Light Industries Co., only one enterprise had a paid-up capital of over I.D. 200,000. On the other hand most of the enterprises in which the Bank participated before 1958 were large enterprises; some of them had a paid-up capital of more than I.D. 2 millions. These are the first 13 enterprises in Table V.12.

FINANCIAL INSTITUTIONS AND INDUSTRIALIZATION

TABLE V.11

Number of Companies in which the Bank Participated
and Value of its Shares
1950–65

Year	No.	I.D.
1950	6	629,272
1951	7	911,482
1952	10	995,281
1953	11	1,139,031
1954	13	1,631,481
1955	14	1,674,756
1956	14	1,896,458
1957	14	1,917,467
1958	14	1,923,270
1959	14	1,423,275
1960	15	1,589,872
1961	16	1,980,520
1962	16	1,995,221
1963	16	2,188,101
1964	4	147,372
1965	7	365,433

Source: The Industrial Bank, *Annual Reports*, 1961–64, p. 12 and 1965, p. 11

TABLE V.12

Companies in which the Industrial Bank was a Shareholder in July 1964

I.D.

Name of Company	Nominal Capital 1	Paid-up Capital 2	Paid by Bank 3	% of Bank Partici- pation 4
Iraq Cement Co.	2,625,000	2,625,000	509,340	19·4
Vegetable Oil Extraction Co.	2,000,000	2,000,000	410,715	20·5
National Leather Industries	500,000	500,000	179,168	42·5
Iraq Spinning and Weaving	1,200,000	1,200,000	425,110	35·4
Iraq Grain Milling Co.	250,000	232,310	60,000	26·4
Iraq Jute Industries	850,000	760,109	127,500	15·0
The Estate Industries	500,000	448,589	100,000	20.0
National Insurance Co.	1,000,000	330,000	45,000	15·0
Iraq Marble Co.	200,000	50,000	10,000	20·0
River Dredging and Land Reclamation	250,000	60,000	15,625	6·2
Iraq Gypsum	150,000	147,291	30,000	20·0
Baghdad Bakery Co.	130,000	129,524	32,500	25·0
Iraq Date Industries	100,000	60,000	10,000	20·0
Re-insurance Co.	5,000,000	1,250,000	100,000	8·0
Light Industries Co.	1,000,000	445,118	62,535	12·5
Amara Industries	100,000	69,414	45,843	49·0
National Chemical Industries Co.	150,000	75,000	17,175	22·9
Total		10,384,355	2,240,511	

Source: Industrial Bank, *Annual Report*, 1961–64, p. 12

98 ROLE OF GOVERNMENT IN INDUSTRIALIZATION OF IRAQ

TABLE V.13

*The Industrial Bank's Participation in Industrial Companies,
December 1965*

I.D.

Name of Company	Nominal Capital	Paid-up Capital	Paid by the Bank	% of Bank's Partici- pation 3–2
	1	*2*	*3*	*4*
Light Industries Co.	1,000,000	527,057	136,410	25·9
Amara Industries Co.	100,000	81,912	48,091	58·7
National Chemical Industries	150,000	75,000	30,057	40·0
Iraq Bicycle Co.	250,000	50,000	31,875	63·7
Northern Wood Co.	150,000	150,000	50,000	33·3
Al-Hilal Industries Co.	210,000	210,000	54,000	25·7
Date Industries Co.	100,000	60,910	15,000	24·6
Total	1,960,000	1,154,879	365,433	31·6

Source: Industrial Bank, *Annual Report*, 1965, p. 11

The failure of the Bank to persuade the private sector to set up large scale companies can partly be explained by the hesitation of the private sector to invest in industry on a large scale after the Revolution of 1958 and its fear of nationalization. Furthermore, after the 'Socialist Laws of 1964', contrary to the previous policy whereby the Bank refrained from holding a majority of shares of industrial enterprises,[49] the Bank started to hold the majority shareholding. Thus it decided to increase its participation in the Light Industries Co., 'in order to increase public control over the activities of that enterprise',[50] and it increased its share in the paid-up capital of that company from 12% in 1964 to 25.9% in 1965.[51] The Bank also created the Iraq Bicycle Co., and retained more than 50% of the shares.[52] When the public was invited to subscribe, the response was disappointing. At that time I was Acting Director of the Economic Department in the Ministry of Industry and in direct contact with many private industrialists. Many of them did not participate in that company because they lacked confidence in an industrial enterprise controlled by the Government. Their fears were soon justified when it was decided, for political reasons, that the plant should be established in a town which lacked almost all basic elements of social overhead capital. But if the Bank wanted to attract the private sector into mixed public and private industrial enterprises, it would be more likely to succeed by going back to the old policy of refraining from hold-

FINANCIAL INSTITUTIONS AND INDUSTRIALIZATION 99

ing the majority of shares of such companies, especially in view of its limited financial resources.

Some observers have argued that the Bank unduly emphasized profitability when it participated in industrial enterprises. Most of the projects in which it held shares were very profitable. The main objective of the Bank, they argue, was to create and assist industries and in certain cases 'this may well mean industries which are unable to make any significant profits but which instead give a general assistance to the whole economy of Iraq'.[53] The World Bank Mission advised the Industrial Bank that 'while it should presumably show a small profit to inspire confidence in its operations, it should not retain its participation in profit making enterprises for the sake of maximising its profits, particularly when this limits its ability to assist other enterprises'.[54] Had the Bank followed this advice it could have turned over its capital far more quickly and increased its activities. More important such a policy could have contributed to the extension of Iraq's primitive capital market by making Iraqis accustomed to holding shares and other securities. The Bank, however, preferred the far less sensible policy of making profits, and only on two occasions did it sell some of its shares in an enterprise.[55]

Technical Assistance: The final and important function of the Bank was to provide technical assistance on economic, engineering, administrative and accounting problems and to prepare feasibility studies for industrial firms. Even in highly industrialized countries it is necessary to supply such assistance to new and expanding enterprises. Unfortunately, the Bank had only a small economic and technical staff which could not provide professional advice on these matters. Thus in 1959 the Bank reported that it could not provide such services,[56] but it hoped to extend technical assistance in the future.[57] By 1966, however, the Technical Department of the Bank consisted of statistical, engineering and economic sections. The engineering section included two civil engineers—one worked full time on a housing scheme for the Bank's staff and the other on the evaluation of property submitted by the Bank's clients as collateral. The statistical section included four graduates, all fully engaged in the preparation of the Bank's annual and monthly reports containing the statistics pertaining to the operations of the Bank. The economic section included beside myself three graduates from the Baghdad College of Commerce. The section was engaged in preparing preliminary reports on loan applications. In early 1965 the Bank was asked by the Ministry of Industry to prepare a prefeasibility study about a car assembly project based on reports presented by a number of motor car manufacturers. By mid-1966

100 ROLE OF GOVERNMENT IN INDUSTRIALIZATION OF IRAQ

nothing of practical value had been achieved and at that time a United Nations expert prepared, in less than a month, a report which exhausted all available information and which contained definite recommendations. Furthermore, the Bank has spent only very small amounts of money on technical research. For example, the amount of expenditure for this purpose was nil for the years 1962, 1963 and 1965, but I.D. 1,820 was spent in 1961 and only I.D. 124 was spent in 1964 compared with a total administrative expenditure of more than I.D. 100,000 per year.[58]

In most developing countries there is usually a shortage of well prepared projects, which reflects the shortage of entrepreneurial skills.[59] Iraq was no exception in this respect. The Bank carried out preliminary work on about 30 projects up to the end of 1965,[60] but it should have taken far more initiative in the exploration of industrial possibilities, particularly in the field of small and medium-sized industries because there was no other Government agency which did this kind of work, and the Ministry of Industry concentrated on the large industrial projects of the public sector for which it hired foreign consultants to prepare the required studies.

REFERENCES

1. Ministry of Guidance, Law No. 87, 1965 for the 1965–66 plan, p. 16
2. Law No. 34, 1950
3. U.N., *Financing of Manufacturing Industry*, p. 18
4. *Ibid.*, p. 22
5. See Table V.3
6. Bates, *The Finance of Small Business*, p. 114
7. Information provided by the Director of the London Branch of Iraq's Rafidain Bank
8. Industrial Bank *Annual Report*, 1961–64, p. 4; and 1965 p. 2
9. Arthur D. Little, *A Plan for Industrial Development In Iraq*, p. 372
10. al-Atrash, *Monetary Policy in an Underdeveloped Economy, with Special Reference to the Experience of Egypt, Iraq and Syria, 1951–58*, p. 93. According to Articles 2 and 8 of Law No. 34 of 1950 for the control of banking, commercial banks were not required to keep reserves with the Central Bank against Government deposits
11. As defined by the Central Bank, *Bulletin, New Series*, No. 1, 1965, p. 25
12. Law No. 34, 1947
13. Law No. 34 of 1950 for the Control of Banking
14. Qaisi, *Iraq's Banking System after Nationalization*, p. 9
15. Central Bank, *Bulletin, New Series*, No. 4, 1967, p. 11
16. See Table V.3
17. Asseily, *A Central Bank for Lebanon*, p. 179
18. Sayers, *Central Banking after Bagehot*, p. 121 and Nevin, *Capital Funds in Underdeveloped Countries*, p. 49
19. Law No. 35 of 1935
20. Industrial Bank, *A Report*, May 1962, p. 2
21. Law No. 124 of 1940
22. Laws, No. 33 of 1935; No. 12 of 1940; No. 87 of 1956 and No. 62 of 1961

FINANCIAL INSTITUTIONS AND INDUSTRIALIZATION 101

23. al-Dally, *Problems of Industrial Enterprise in Iraq*, p. 44 and note 23, p. 19
24. Law No. 99 of 1964
25. The Industrial Bank, *Annual Report*, March 1965, p. 19
26. *Ibid.*, p. 2
27. *Ibid.*, p. 2 and the Industrial Bank, *Comment on the Five-Year Plan 1965–69*, pp. 15–16
28. See Table III.5
29. See Tables IV.1 and IV.2
30. The Industrial Bank, *Comment on the Five-Year Plan, 1965–69*, p. 14
31. Law No. 62, of 1961
32. Law No. 31, 1961 and No. 164, 1964
33. The Industrial Bank, *A Report*, March 1965, p. 7
34. Langley, *Industrialization of Iraq*, p. 148
35. This can be appreciated from Table III.11, and the fact that about 60% of the Bank's credit went to textiles, food, drink, and similar enterprises. Industrial Bank, *Annual Reports*, 1961–64, p. 16, 1965, p. 22
36. Industrial Bank, *Annual Report*, 1965, p. 28
37. Industrial Bank, *Annual Reports*, 1961–64, p. 4 and 1965, p. 5
38. The Industrial Bank, *A Report*, March, 1965, p. 4
39. Law No. 62 of 1961
40. The Industrial Bank, *A Report*, March, 1965, p. 7
41. See Table V.6
42. The Industrial Bank *Annual Report*, 1965, p. 2
43. These rates are given by the Industrial Bank, *A Report*, March, 1965, p. 7
44. I.B.R.D., *Economic Development of Iraq*, p. 33
45. Laws No. 12 of 1940 and No. 87 of 1956
46. al-Jalili, *Lectures on Economics of Iraq*, p. 220
47. Law No. 62, of 1961
48. See Table V.11
49. See Table V.12
50. Industrial Bank, *Annual Report*, 1965, p. 9
51. Tables V.12 and V.13
52. Industrial Bank, *Annual Report*, 1965, p. 7
53. Iversen, *Monetary Policy in Iraq*, p. 33
54. I.B.R.D., *Economic Development of Iraq*, p. 40
55. The Industrial Bank, *A Report*, March, 1965, p. 4
56. Industrial Bank, *Annual Report*, 1958–59, p. 3
57. Government of Iraq, *The Revolution, in its First Year*, p. 37
58. Industrial Bank, *Annual Reports*, 1961–64, p. 11 and 1965, p. 36
59. U.N., *Process and Problems of Industrialization in Underdeveloped Countries*, pp. 56–57
60. The Industrial Bank, *A Report*, March 1965, p. 3

H

Chapter VI

OTHER POLICIES TO PROMOTE INDUSTRIALIZATION: PROTECTION, TAX EXEMPTION, AND CONTROL OF PRIVATE INVESTMENT

The Government sought to promote the growth of private industry in three ways : (1) through protection from foreign competition by tariffs and quotas, (2) through tax exemption of all kinds designed to encourage private investment in industry and (3) through controls over the allocation of private investment in industry. This chapter will outline, analyse, and appraise each of these policies.

1. *Protection*

In Iraq two cases have been made for protection, one related to the saving in foreign exchange and the other was based on the infant industry argument. I propose to discuss these in turn.

The balance of trade argument has been used as a major justification for protection. The argument focusses upon the deficit in the trade balance, excluding oil, and concludes that this must be remedied because 'the development of any country on a sound basis makes it necessary to change the trade balance in its favour by increasing exports and decreasing imports'.[1] This argument may be dismissed, for the country's balance of payment excluding oil is of no relevance. Oil revenues provided Iraq with foreign exchange equivalent to about 20% of her national income during the period 1950–65 on average, and they represented 83% of Iraq's foreign exchange earnings during the same period. The country did not experience balance of payment difficulties and protection can hardly be justified on the ground that it preserved scarce foreign exchange.

The infant industry argument was accepted in Iraq almost as a matter of faith. 'Protection of infant industries is necessary', stated the Ministry of Industry, 'because of the dumping policies practised by advanced countries and designed to destroy infant industries in countries like Iraq, and because local industries cannot compete with foreign large scale enterprises which have long industrial ex-

OTHER POLICIES TO PROMOTE INDUSTRIALIZATION 103

perience'.[2] The modern version of the infant industry argument runs in terms of prices which do not reflect long run social costs and benefits. While it is true that when a country specializes according to its comparative advantage and trades at international exchange ratios, its gain is similar to a shift in its production possibility curve, the core of the infant industry argument is that a different pattern of resource allocation will bring about a greater and irreversible shift of the curve itself. This is due to the possibility that when an industry is protected, skills will be acquired and the industry will be able to produce at lower costs as a result of full exploitation of the economies of scale. Yet to evaluate infant industries is extremely difficult. Moreover if an infant industry is to mature it must not only become efficient, but also realize a sufficient saving in costs to compensate for the higher costs of infancy.[3]

The cost of protection is an important practical question because the ease with which policy makers in Iraq resorted to trade controls suggests that they regarded trade restrictions as almost costless. These restrictions—tariffs, for example—tend to increase home production, decrease imports and reduce consumption. Their costs to the economy can be divided into two elements—the consumption cost equal to the loss of consumer surplus which arises from distortions in the pattern of trade and from higher prices, and production costs equal to the extra cost of producing additional amounts of the protected goods domestically.[4] Both consumption and production costs tend to be relatively high in small poor countries due to their relatively inflexible economic structure, low elasticities of substitution among consumer goods and high dependence on trade.[5]

The practical argument for protecting an infant industry depends on whether the cost of adopting the policy is greater or less than the benefits claimed for that policy. If future savings compensate for initial losses, there is no prolonged need for protection because the industry will be profitable over its whole life span. Nevertheless investors may not have foresight to realize this, or the long run may be too long, and there is need for public intervention. The justification for protection is stronger if the industry creates external economies. Here we have a divergence between private and social costs and protection is justified to correct the market mechanism. Some economists believe that these economies are more important in the industrial sector than in other sectors and to ignore them is likely to bias resource allocation against industry.[6] Others stress the difficulties of measuring these economies and maintain that they 'might be substantial in the export sector, domestic industry or in public overhead capital'.[7] Despite these limitations and

104 ROLE OF GOVERNMENT IN INDUSTRIALIZATION OF IRAQ

qualifications, most people accept the general case for protection on the basis of the infant industry argument.

Given a case for intervention in international trade, a variety of controls can be used. Controls on imports can operate through multiple exchange rates (which make some uses of money more expensive than others), through import quotas and prohibitions, tariffs and subsidies. The Government of Iraq has used tariffs, quotas and import prohibitions to make protection effective, and I will confine my discussion to these techniques.

The Tariff System: The basis of Iraq's tariff system was established during the Mandate (1921–32) and can be found in Tariff Proclamation No. 19, 1919 which levied an ad valorem rate of 11% on all imports, with the exception of tobacco, alcoholic liquors and perfumes which were subject to specific rates of duty equivalent to 50% of their value.[8] Subsequent amendments raised ad valorem rates and made most of Iraq's imports subject to specific rates of tax. While the typical ad valorem rate was 15%, specific rates varied from 25% on metals up to 100% or more on tea, matches, sugar, cigarettes and alcohol.[9]

Up to 1927 tariffs were designed to collect revenues but Law No. 20 of that year exempted from customs duty most machinery and raw materials required for industry, agriculture and construction.[10] Immediately after independence the Government promulgated Law No. 11 of 1933. This law included all the exemptions cited above and imposed specific duties on the most important imports. Rates of duty rose with the degree of processing involved in imported commodities. Necessities were taxed at lower rates and higher rates were imposed on imports which competed with domestic industry.[11]

Tariff Law No. 77 of 1955 replaced the 1933 law but went further in the application of the principles of the 1933 law. It covered nearly 1,500 items against 414 in the previous law. It exempted from duty 177 commodities compared to 137 in 1933. These commodities included raw materials and machinery. The average rate on imported unprocessed goods was reduced from 22% to 15%. The new law also reduced duties on some consumer goods, such as tea and sugar, by 10%, and it increased protective duties on goods produced locally like cement, soap, shoes, vegetable oils, dairy products, cotton and woollen piece goods. But in general the level of duty was reduced.[12]

Up to the end of the financial year 1965 this law had been amended several times. Of importance was Law No. 30 of 1962 which enlarged the number of commodities exempted from customs duty, such as raw materials and machinery, increased duty on luxury

OTHER POLICIES TO PROMOTE INDUSTRIALIZATION   105

goods, especially consumer durables, and duties on commodities which competed with domestic industry. The aim of the tariff system was still to collect revenue and protect local industries.[13]

Revenue Aspects of the Tariff: Since the establishment of Iraqi Government in 1921, import duties have been an important source of tax revenue. The share of import duties in total Government revenues increased from 31% in 1921 to 40% in 1930. Then it declined to 28% in 1939 and 26% in 1949.[14] During the period 1950–65 the ratio of import duties to total Government revenues declined from 27% in 1950 to 12% in 1965.[15] The main reason for the decline in the importance of import duties was the rapid rise in oil revenues. Since 1950 Iraq's Development Budget has been financed almost entirely from oil revenues. If, however, we consider the Ordinary Budget alone (without oil revenues), the share of import duties increased from 33% in 1950 to 49% in 1955, then the ratio declined to 27% in 1965. The share of import duties in the Ordinary Budget including oil revenues rose from 27% in 1950 to 34% in 1957. When the percentage of oil revenues allocated to the Ordinary Budget rose from 30% to 50% after 1958, the relative importance of import duties declined to 16% in 1965.[16] These duties were still important, and their contribution to total tax income of the Government was 50% in that year; they were the most important single source of tax revenue after taxes on oil.[17]

The heavy emphasis on import duties as a source of tax revenue has been noticed in other poor countries, mainly because it is administratively easier to tax commodities than income, and goods which flow through a few points of entry or exit to a country can be more readily taxed than commodities produced and distributed internally. In Iraq oil revenues have diminished the importance of import duties as a source of public finance. They nevertheless remain significant, and the actual administration of the tariff, as well as tariff policy, was still in 1965 the responsibility of the Ministry of Finance.

Protective Aspects of the Tariff: A tariff designed only to raise revenue must be levied on goods not produced domestically or on goods on which an equal tax is imposed on domestic production to eliminate the protective aspect. Less rigid definitions might include as revenue duties all levies which are too low to protect a local product, and those which are exceptionally high, such as those applying to alcoholic liquors and matches, while the excise duties on domestically produced products are far too small to balance the import duty.[18] In between there are rates obviously protective.

The 1933 law encouraged industry mainly by levying low duties on inputs, but it protected local industry by levying high duties on

TABLE VI.1
Import Duties as a Source of Government Revenue, 1950–65
I.D. Million

Year	Import Duty 1	Ordinary Budget Revenue 2	Development Budget Revenue 3	2+3 4	Oil Revenue 5	Share of Oil Revenue in Ordinary Budget 6	Share of Oil in Development Budget 7	Ordinary Budget Revenue other than Oil 8	1 as % of 4 9	1 as % of 2 10	1 as % of 8 11
1950	9·2	33·2	0·3	33·5	5·6	5·2	0·3	28·0	27	27	33
1951	11·0	37·5	7·5	45·0	13·9	3·1	7·4	34·3	24	29	32
1952	11·2	50·5	23·9	74·4	40·1	9·5	23·9	41·0	15	22	27
1953	14·6	47·7	35·3	83·0	58·3	15·0	35·3	32·7	18	31	45
1954	16·6	52·2	40·7	93·0	68·4	17·1	40·7	35·0	18	32	47
1955	19·7	65·3	60·8	126·1	73·7	25·3	60·8	39·9	16	30	49
1956	19·4	62·7	51·1	113·8	68·8	20·6	51·1	42·0	17	31	46
1957	21·1	61·9	35·9	97·8	48·8	14·6	35·9	47·2	22	34	45
1958	19·1	75·6	61·7	137·3	79·9	26·0	61·7	49·5	14	25	39
1959	19·7	89·7	43·6	133·3	86·6	43·3	43·5	46·4	15	22	42
1960	24·6	103·6	47·7	151·3	95·0	47·5	47·6	56·0	16	24	44
1961	24·4	120·7	66·7	187·4	94·8	58·1	66·7	62·5	13	20	39
1962	23·6	114·7	70·0	184·7	95·1	48·5	70·0	66·2	13	21	36
1963	22·3	127·8	67·6	195·4	110·0	57·2	67·6	69·5	11	17	32
1964	26·1	143·1	66·6	209·7	126·1	64·8	66·6	78·3	12	18	33
1965	28·8	177·0	70·8	247·8	135·4	67·7	67·7	109·3	12	16	26

Source: Column 1: as in table VI.2, column 6
Column 2: Central Bank of Iraq, *Bulletin, New Series*, No. 1, 1965, p. 30 and No. 3, 1967, p. 24 and Ministry of Finance, Department of Accounts, *Annual Report*, 1959, p. 61
Column 3: Central Bank of Iraq, *Bulletin, New Series*, No. 1, 1965, p. 33 and No. 3, 1967, p. 27
Column 5: Iraq Petroleum Company, Oil Information and Statistics Section, *Report on the Operation of Oil Companies*, 12 April, 1966, p. 13, and Central Bank of Iraq, *Bulletin New Series*, No. 3, 1967, pp. 25, 28
Columns 6 and 7: Central Bank of Iraq, *Quarterly Bulletin*, No. 59, p. 43, Ministry of Finance, Department of Accounts, *Annual Reports*, 1961, p. 78 and 1963, p. 87; Central Bank of Iraq, *Bulletin, New Series*, No. 3, 1967, pp. 25, 28

OTHER POLICIES TO PROMOTE INDUSTRIALIZATION 107

a few commodities. This was 'inevitable because there were only a few worthwhile industrial projects to be protected'.[19] The 1955 tariff law and its amendments in 1962 increased the extent of protection considerably. Can this be quantified?

Several authorities have related the amount of revenue collected to the total value of imports and found that the average tariff rose from 10% in 1921 to 34% in 1933, remained stable till 1939, declined sharply during the war and increased to the pre-war level by 1950. Since then the ratio declined to 16% in 1965.[20] These figures are misleading because they relate tariff revenues to total imports including those commodities which pay no duty. Although the Government reduced some duties, for example those on sugar and tea, by 10%, this does not explain the whole decline in the average tariff ratio since 1950. There are other reasons for the fall. One is the fact that most of the important imports were taxed on a specific basis which means that increased import prices produced a fall in the ad valorem rate of duty.[21] Another reason is the shift in the pattern of Iraq's imports from consumer goods towards capital goods; that is, a shift towards commodities which paid little or no duty. From 1950 to 1965 the percentage of capital goods in total imports rose from 17% to 50%.[22] At the same time imports by industrial enterprises exempted from import duties increased both in absolute terms and as a percentage of total capital goods imports. If we exclude imports of industrial enterprises, the average tariff rises to 19% in 1965, compared with 16% on the simple average. The remainder of capital goods paid duty up to 10% ad valorem. Assuming that on the average this rate amounted to 5% we can take out capital goods from the total imports and take out duties paid on capital goods. We are then left with a value of imports other than capital goods and the relevant amount of duty. On this basis the average tariffs will rise to 26% in 1965.[23] This ratio still includes pure revenue tariffs and it takes no account of goods not imported because of duties. My figures seem a more satisfactory measure than the crude average, and one can estimate the potential rate of protection at between 25–30%.

The compilation of a more refined ratio which takes into account the sums collected on low revenue duties, exceptionally high revenue duties, goods not produced in Iraq, etc., would be laborious. Furthermore, if one is interested in the actual rate of protection extended by the Government an aggregate approach is unsatisfactory. One should concentrate on industry alone. But to prepare an index containing all import competing items, would be impracticable and one is faced immediately with the sampling problem. Moreover, most competing industrial goods are not included

TABLE VI.2

Protective Aspects of Tariffs
The Simple and the Refined Average Tariffs, 1950–65

I.D. Million

Year	Imports Other than Imports by Oil Companies 1	Imports of Capital Goods 2	Imports by Industrial Enterprise Exempted from Duty 3	Imports Other than Capital Goods 1–2 4	Capital Goods Minus Imports by Industry 2–3 5	Import Duties 6	The Simple Average Tariff 6 as % of 1 7	6 as % of 4 8	Imports Minus Imports by Industry 1–3 9	6 as % of 9 10	Imports Duties Minus Duties on Capital Goods 11	The Refined Average Tariff 12
1950	29.2	5.0	1.0	24.2	4.0	9.2	31	38	28.2	33	9.0	37
1951	42.2	11.4	1.7	30.8	9.7	11.0	26	36	40.5	27	9.2	30
1952	47.7	15.7	2.8	32.0	12.9	11.2	23	35	44.9	25	10.5	33
1953	55.5	23.0	4.4	32.5	18.6	14.6	26	45	51.1	28	13.7	42
1954	68.3	30.4	4.0	37.9	26.4	16.6	24	44	64.3	26	15.3	40
1955	90.9	45.1	4.6	45.8	40.5	19.7	22	47	86.3	23	17.7	39
1956	107.2	55.2	9.4	52.0	45.8	19.4	18	37	97.8	20	17.2	33
1957	112.0	45.7	15.4	66.3	40.3	21.1	19	32	96.6	24	19.1	29
1958	99.8	43.1	11.6	56.7	31.5	19.1	19	34	88.2	22	18.7	33
1959	99.4	37.0	19.9	62.4	17.1	19.7	20	32	79.5	25	18.9	30
1960	124.3	44.0	17.4	80.3	26.6	24.6	20	31	106.9	23	23.3	29
1961	133.5	48.6	15.8	84.9	32.8	24.4	18	29	117.7	21	22.8	27
1962	127.7	53.5	14.9	74.2	38.6	23.6	18	32	112.8	21	21.7	29
1963	112.5	49.3	15.1	63.2	31.2	22.3	20	34	97.4	25	20.8	31
1964	146.7	56.8	23.9	89.9	32.9	26.1	18	29	122.8	21	24.5	27
1965	159.9	69.4	25.2	90.5	44.2	28.8	18	28	134.7	21	23.6	26

Source: Column 1: Central Bank of Iraq, *Bulletin*, 1965, New Series, No. 1, p. 48

Column 2: Table VI.5, column 3

Column 3: Ministry of Planning, Central Bureau of Statistics, *Statistical Abstract*, 1965, p. 237, 1961, p. 235, 1958, p. 192

Column 6: Central Bank of Iraq, *Quarterly Bulletin*, No. 59, 1965, p. 43 and *Bulletin*, New Series, No. 4, 1967, p. 25; Ministry of Finance Department of Accounts, *Annual Reports*, 1959, p. 78 and 1960, p. 73

OTHER POLICIES TO PROMOTE INDUSTRIALIZATION 109

separately in Iraq's statistics of foreign trade. Finally, even if these difficulties could be overcome the average tariff index on competing industrial goods would not measure the extent of protection, because tariffs were supplemented by quotas and prohibitions.

As an approximation I have calculated the extent of tariff protection on more than 30 imported industrial products with domestically produced substitutes, excluding commodities such as non-alcoholic beverages, bricks, tiles, perishable products protected by transport costs, and high revenue items such as sugar, alcoholic liquors, cigarettes, matches, etc. From this Table VI.3 was constructed, which shows that the simple average rate was 33% in 1956 but increased to 51% in 1962. This is not a satisfactory average. Ideally the restrictive effect of the tariff should be weighted by 'the difference between hypothetical imports in the absence of tariff and actual imports'.[24] It is not possible to get such an index. Nor can a satisfactory index be obtained if each tariff is weighed by the value of actual imports, because when tariffs are increased and imports fall more than proportionately, the weighted mean of the tariff falls and this, needless to say, misrepresents the comparative restrictiveness of the tariff before and after the change in the rates. In the absence of 'a more appropriate system of weighting . . . the use of the unweighted mean tariff as a measure of the degree of restrictiveness of a given national tariff structure seems more justified, and has been generally adopted by the E.E.C. authorities'.[25] I did not find it necessary to calculate a weighted average for my purpose. It is enough to notice that the rate varied from 17% to more than 100%. Thus, the actual tariff protection was, at least in some cases, substantially higher than indicated by the previous index (25–30%) derived from an aggregate approach. It seems that tariff policy makers were prepared to increase the rate when an industry was established or expanded but tariffs were rarely raised to prohibitive levels. As the 1962 amendment mentions, tariff rates were kept down in order to permit a limited amount of imports to compete with domestic products and to provide revenue for the Treasury.[26]

Are these rates excessive? There is no satisfactory answer to such a question but it is interesting to notice that Friedrich List regarded a manufacturing industry that could not survive on 20–30% tariff as unsuitable for the country. Such rates, according to Professor Haberler, have 'to be regarded as very moderate nowadays'.[27] Most rates in Iraq stood at 30% or less (18 out of 33 items in 1962 and 22 from 33 in 1956). It seems that Iraq's tariff rates can be described as relatively 'moderate'.

One important qualification concerns the duties levied on raw

110 ROLE OF GOVERNMENT IN INDUSTRIALIZATION OF IRAQ

TABLE VI.3

Average Tariff Rates on Selected Imports Competing Commodities 1956 and 1962

Tariff Code	Commodity	1956 Specific Rate	1956 Ad valorem Rate	1962 Specific Rate	1962 Ad valorem Rate
25.23.a	Cement	2 f/k	10	3 f/k	18
73.36.a	Oil heaters		15		20
73.31.b	Nails exceeding 2 centimetres	8 f/k	12	15 f/k	24
48.14	Paper bags	20 f/k	8		25
68.12.a	Asbestos pipes, etc.	4 f/k	20		25
84.12.b	Air coolers		20		25
84.17.b	Water heaters		15		25
82.11	Razor blades		20		25
48.18	Stationery, paper and books		15		25
73.13.a	Nails not exceeding 2 centimetres	16 f/k	8		27
41.2.b	Leather other than sole leather	350 f/k	20		30
44.23	Builders carpentry	30 f/k	9		30
44.24	Household utensils of wood	30 f/k	8		30
62.2.c	Cotton bed linen		25		30
73.35	Iron and steel springs		15		30
48.15.b	Toilet papers		15		30
53.11	Woollen textiles		27		35
61.1	Outer garments		30		35
58.1	Wool carpets		25		40
61.3.4	Undergarments knitted		32		41
60.3	Stockings		40		45
41.2.a	Sole leather	180 f/k	40		50
34.2	Detergents		20		50
62.01	Woollen Blankets	300 f/k	30		60
18.6	Chocolate		50	225 f/k	70
34.1.c.1	Toilet Soap	60 f/k	30	150 f/k	80
33.b.c.2	Cosmetics		50		100
94.1	Furniture		32		100
15.13.a	Vegetable oils	100 f/k	83	100 f/k	110
20.3.b.2	Jams, jellies, etc.	60 f/k	90	100 f/k	114
17.4	Sugar confectionery	150 f/k	100	225 f/k	120
76.15	Household utensils of aluminium	90 f/k	170	90 f/k	176
Average			33		51

Notes: (1) F/k means fils per kilogramme
(2) I chose these products with the help of Mr. M. M. al-Baya, head of the Marketing Section in the Centre for Development of Industrial Management of the Ministry of Industry. The relevant tariff rates are from Tariff Law of 1955 and its amendment in 1962. I transformed the specific rates into ad valorem rates on the basis of the values of actual imports according to the statistics of foreign trade in relevant years as published by the Ministry of Planning, Central Bureau of Statistics. In terms of value of output these industries represented 25% of the whole industrial sector in 1962, Central Bureau of Statistics, *Industrial Census*, 1962, pp. 14–17

OTHER POLICIES TO PROMOTE INDUSTRIALIZATION 111

materials, machinery and other capital imports. Most of these enter Iraq duty free or at lower rates than those levied on finished goods. Under these circumstances 'effective protection' must be higher than the apparent rate. The concept of effective protection relates the amount of duty on the imported product to the value added in the import competing industry. For example, if the tariff on nylon stockings is 55% and on nylon thread 20%, and if, in the absence of a tariff, thread constitutes 50% of the value of the stocking, the effective rate, according to Cordon's method[28] will be: $(0.55 — 0.20) (0.50) \div (1 — 0.50) = 90\%$. This follows because we relate the duty on the nylon stocking to the value added in the domestic industry which imports nylon thread.

To calculate effective protection one has to know import content per unit of production, the duty on imported inputs and then relate this to duty on the finished imports. For Iraq such data are scarce and the problem is further complicated by the Laws for Industrial Encouragement. Under these laws industrial enterprises were entitled to import some or all of their machinery, spare parts, raw materials, etc., duty free but the required information is not published. In general, however, the higher the cost of imports per unit of output the greater the effective rate will be for any nominal tariff rate. All industries listed in Table VI.3 import machinery and spare parts, and most of them import a considerable amount of their raw materials. In most cases the value added in Iraq is small compared to the cost of imports, because the domestic processing is of the 'finishing touch' type, accordingly one can assume that the effective rates are substantially higher than the apparent rates of tariff protection.

Quota Restriction: The second amendment to the 1933 tariff law and article seven of the 1955 law authorized the Government to regulate the imports of any commodity in respect either of quantity or value. During the war imports of all goods became subject to licences but after the war these quantitative restrictions were gradually relaxed.[29] By 1948 as a result of Iraq's widening deficit in the balance of payments, imports of all goods were again made subject to licences. The Government drew up an import programme which gave priority to essential capital and consumer goods. From 1952–58, with increased supplies of foreign exchange these regulations lapsed. Import licences were issued liberally while raw materials and machinery were exempted from quota licensing entirely.[30]

After the Revolution of 1958, in accordance with the 'principle of regulating the use of foreign exchange according to national interests',[31] imports of all goods became again subject to licence.

112 ROLE OF GOVERNMENT IN INDUSTRIALIZATION OF IRAQ

The objectives of the Iraqi quota system can be divided into measures to control overall imports in order to reduce the deficit in the trade balance, and measures to effect the composition of imports designed either to protect selected industries or to encourage the import of capital goods at the expense of consumer goods.[32]

The balance of trade argument has been used as a major justification for import control. But the country experienced no balance of payment difficulties during the period 1950–65.

Although policy makers justified quotas on the grounds that they preserved scarce foreign exchange, Table VI.4 reveals the weakness of this argument. From 1952–58 the value of licences issued fell below actual imports, because licences were not required for the importation of a wide range of commodities,[33] and when licences were required the issue was liberal. In fact the value of the licences issued for most licensed goods was greater than actual imports.[34]

TABLE VI.4

Value of Import Licences Issued and Value of Actual Imports

I.D. Millions

Year	Imports other than Imports by Oil Companies	Import Licences	2–1
1950	29·2	53·5	+ 24·3
1951	42·2	62·7	+ 20·5
1952	47·4	48·8	+ 1·4
1953	55·5	14·7	− 40·8
1954	68·3	19·4	− 48·9
1955	90·9	23·1	− 67·8
1956	107·2	22·6	− 84·6
1957	112·0	26·2	− 85·8
1958	99·8	77·5	− 22·3
1959	99·4	167·7	+ 68·3
1960	124·5	154·5	+ 30·2
1961	133·5	148·3	+ 14·8
1962	127·7	160·6	+ 32·9
1963	112·5	126·6	+ 14·1
1964	146·7	n.a.	n.a.
1965	159·9	133·5	− 26·4

Source: Imports—From Central Bank, *Bulletin, New Series*, 1965, No. 1, p. 48; Import Licences—From Ministry of Planning, Central Bureau of Statistics, *Statististical Abstracts*, and Central Bank, *Quarterly Bulletins*, for the years 1950–65

Notes: The decline in value of licences from 1952 was due to abolition of licence requirements on a number of imported goods. National Bank of Iraq (called Central Bank from 1956), *Quarterly Bulletin*, No. 8, 1953, p. 17
In case of discrepancy between figures, the latest figure was taken
n.a. = not available

OTHER POLICIES TO PROMOTE INDUSTRIALIZATION 113

From 1959 all imports were licensed but the value of licences issued exceeded the value of imports[35] and in 1965 when 'the quota was set at a low level . . . in view of the exhaustion of appropriations for certain items . . . an amount of I.D. 13 million was added'.[36] The data available shows that the quota system, misleadingly called import programmes, was not effectively used to control overall imports.

The quota system sought to encourage the import of capital goods. Table VI.5 shows that during 1952–58 when investment goods were not subject to quotas, imports of capital goods increased from I.D. 5 million, or 16.7% of total imports, in 1950 to I.D. 43 million, or 45% of the total imports in 1958. Then imports became subject to licence from 1959 and the value of capital good imports fell to I.D. 37 million in that year (37% of total imports); not until 1965 did the absolute amount of capital goods attain the peak total of 1956. Thus despite the quota system's bias in favour of capital goods the import of these goods declined because the import of capital goods depends on too many factors beside quota restrictions. When foreign exchange is scarce, quotas can be used to facilitate the import of capital goods in preference to other commodities, but in Iraq there was no shortage of foreign exchange hence quotas were neither necessary nor did they increase the import of capital goods.

The final and perhaps most significant justification for the quota system was that it was necessary to protect local industry. Prior to 1959 import policy provided for only mild restrictions on competitive imports. With few exceptions the restrictions were in values —not in physical terms—and values were determined haphazardly on the basis of previous imports. This gave rise to complaints by industrialists and some economists who claimed that restriction by value cannot exclude foreign industrial products because the local importers agreed with foreign suppliers to declare fictitious prices. Foreign producers could also cut prices to enter the protected market on a larger scale.[37]

Import policy from 1959–65 banned imports of goods where productive capacity of domestic industry was sufficient for local needs; where local needs were estimated to be more than the productive capacity of local industry the quota was set at a level to bridge the gap. Protection through quotas was necessary, according to the Iraqi Ministry of Industry, to prevent dumping and to protect infant industries.[38] The question is how far can this argument support a case for quantitive restrictions as compared to the use of tariffs?

If the demand and supply curves for a particular commodity are not perfectly inelastic there is little difference whether tariffs or

TABLE VI.5

Imports of Capital Goods 1950–65

I.D. Millions

Year	Total Imports Other than by Oil Companies 1	Capital Goods Imports* 2	Capital Imports† 3	Consumer Goods Imports* 4	Consumer* Capital Goods Imports 5	Capital Goods Imports† 6	3 as % of 1 7	3 as % of 5 8	6 as % of 1 9
1950	29·2	5·0	5·0	23·5	28·4	5·9	17·1	17·6	20·2
1951	42·2	11·4	11·4	24·2	35·6	9·0	27·0	32·0	21·3
1952	47·4	15·7	15·7	22·6	38·3	13·6	33·1	40·9	28·6
1953	55·5	23·0	23·0	22·3	45·3	20·3	41·4	50·7	36·5
1954	68·3	30·4	30·4	27·4	57·8	24·3	44·5	52·6	35·5
1955	90·9	45·1	45·1	30·7	75·8	35·4	49·6	59·4	38·9
1956	107·2	55·2	55·2	30·5	85·7	43·3	51·5	64·4	40·4
1957	112·0	45·7	45·7	36·4	82·1	40·3	40·8	55·6	35·9
1958	99·8	43·1	43·1	36·2	79·3	39·0	43·2	54·3	39·0
1959	99·4	37·0	37·0	45·5	83·5	32·7	37·2	44·3	32·8
1960	124·3	44·0	44·0	60·8	104·8	40·1	35·3	41·9	32·2
1961	133·5	48·6	48·6	65·2	113·8	43·9	36·4	42·7	32·8
1962	127·7	53·5	53·5	54·3	107·8	48·8	41·8	49·6	38·2
1963	112·5	52·3	46·3	47·8	92·8		41·1	50·0	
1964	146·7	65·0	56·8	66·3	123·1		38·7	46·2	
1965	159·9	74·5	69·4	69·6	139·9		43·4	49·6	

Source: Table VI.4; Central Bank, *Annual Reports*, 1954–65 and *Quarterly Bulletin*, No. 1, p. 19; al-Atraqchi, *Pattern of Merchandise Foreign Trade in Iraq*, 1948–62, p. 165

Notes: Column 3 is the same as in Column 2, except for the years 1963–65. During these years certain items were included by the Central Bank, but I have excluded them to make the figures comparable

* Central Bank estimates
† Dr. Atraqchi's estimates

OTHER POLICIES TO PROMOTE INDUSTRIALIZATION 115

quotas are used to protect an industry provided that the quota is set at the volume of imports which would result from a given tariff. But if there is an inelastic supply of that commodity from outside or if foreign producers dump exports at prices lower than those in the home markets, then a tariff may not increase the price or reduce the volume of imports to the required extent. Under these circumstances quotas should be imposed to restrict imports. The quota can then be justified on the grounds that domestic resources are engaged in the production of the commodity which cannot be temporarily shifted out of the industry concerned and easily be shifted back later.[39]

It is one thing, however, to point out on theoretical basis that quotas are useful because of dumping, but it is an entirely different matter to demonstrate that dumping exists and occurs on a large scale. The Iraqi officials used the dumping argument to support the imposition of quotas but they did not cite any evidence to demonstrate the existence of dumping.

Tariffs are not costless, but quotas are even more expensive for consumers. They are more restrictive and tend to reduce competition and establish monopolies to a larger extent than tariffs. They raise the price of imports and in the absence of the auctioning of import licences, importers may secure for themselves this increase in value due to created scarcity, hence import licences become valuable and this may lead to corruption[40] or if corruption already existed this adds yet another form. Even without corruption there are other difficulties when decisions are taken about quantities of different imports, from where to import and by whom. In taking these decisions administrators are frequently affected by considerations of fairness and other arbitrary personal prejudices.

Our problem is how to evaluate the case for quantitative restriction in Iraq. Unfortunately, only meagre information is available. Until 1961 protection was granted by the Higher Supply Committee —a ministerial committee under the chairmanship of the Prime Minister—on the strength of recommendations of ad hoc committees. Thereafter the Permanent Committee for Protection was established under the Ministry of Trade with a membership drawn from the Ministries of Trade, Industry and Finance, the Federation of Industry and Baghdad Chamber of Commerce.[41] The first wave of quota protection after the Revolution of 1958 came in 1959 when 'imports of some foreign goods were banned . . . while imports of other commodities not manufactured locally in sufficient quantities were limited'.[42] From 1960–65 a further 63 products received protection, 29 were protected by import quotas and 34 items completely protected by import prohibition as can be seen

116   ROLE OF GOVERNMENT IN INDUSTRIALIZATION OF IRAQ

from Table IV.6, which also shows that the range of quota protection was becoming wider.

TABLE VI.6

No. of Industrial Products Completely or Partly Protected by Quotas
1960–65

Year	Partly Protected	Completely Protected	Total
1960	2	6	8
1961	6	4	10
1962	4	4	8
1963	4	5	9
1964	6	3	9
1965	7	12	19
Total	29	34	63

Source: Central Bureau of Statistics, *Statistical Abstract*, 1965, p. 237

No information is published by the Permanent Committee for Protection but according to one member[43] the Committee scrutinized applications for protection by industrialists, collected data from the Ministries of Economy[44] and Industry, the Federation of Industry and Chamber of Commerce. The Committee visited the factories concerned and eventually prepared a small report including recommendations for the Minister of Economy. Usually the Minister accepted the recommendations of the Committee. Protection was granted initially for one year, at the end of which the case was restudied and if the Committee was satisfied protection became permanent.

In fifteen of the reports of the Committee that I have seen, and in the supporting statements prepared for it by the Federation of Industry,[45] decisions in every case were taken on the basis of 'local needs' compared to 'productive capacity of domestic industry'. Local needs were defined as equal to average annual imports plus domestic production sold over the past two or three years. The Committee rarely made projections of future demand or supply. Productive capacity was defined as almost equal to maximum output on the basis of more than one shift of work per day under ideal conditions. Prices used for comparison were wholesale prices in Baghdad of domestic and imported goods. Other Departments were sometimes consulted on questions of quality but in most cases the Committee's decision was based on its own evaluation of whether the available domestic product reached some minimum required standard. If the Committee found that domestic capacity could meet the local needs, that the price of the local product was below or a little higher than the price of the imported substitute and

OTHER POLICIES TO PROMOTE INDUSTRIALIZATION 117

the quality was satisfactory, it recommended permanent import prohibition even if only one local producer operated.

The Committee's method of investigation did not involve any consideration of long run efficiency. It made no attempt to compare domestic costs of production of a commodity with its real cost for the economy. For imported goods Baghdad wholesale prices would be higher than the cost c.i.f., because Baghdad prices include customs duties and reflect the operation of the quota system. The Committee made no attempt to study whether any protected industry might become efficient. It attached little value to competition and displayed no awareness of the disadvantages of monopoly. The following quotations makes official attitudes towards foreign competition all too clear!

The National Bank of Iraq claimed that 'the most important means which must be taken to achieve domestic production and just distribution is the adoption of the principle of quantitative limitation or total prohibition of the import of foreign commodities the competition of which cannot be destroyed in any other way'.[46] 'This Ministry', stated the Ministry of Industry, 'takes care to protect domestic products according to the principle of the domestic market for national products',[47] while the Ministry of Trade stated that 'the basic aims of commercial policy are protection for national industries against foreign competition by prohibiting the import of commodities produced locally and limiting the imports of goods not produced in sufficient amounts to meet market requirements'.[48] As Adams noticed and reports of the Federation of Industry substantiate 'the philosophy of eliminating competition rather than working for efficient production and improved quality is contagious, and is evident in the private sector of the economy also. Private producers come to expect the Government to protect their market by means ranging from high duties to outright prohibition on import competing products.'[49]

It is interesting to see, however, that the Ministry of Finance declared that 'wherever possible it is better to protect by tariffs rather than by quantitative restrictions of imports because the tariff rate, if chosen carefully, can ensure protection of domestic industry as well as other aims which cannot be achieved by quantitative import restrictions or import prohibitions, because imports prevent monopoly, stimulate improvement in quality of domestic products, satisfy consumer demands in a better way, collect revenues for the Treasury and combat inflation'.[50] Why then did the Permanent Committee for Protection resort to quantitative restrictions as the main instrument of protection?

The Ministry of Trade was responsible for import policy and has

I

118   ROLE OF GOVERNMENT IN INDUSTRIALIZATION OF IRAQ

attached to it the Committee for Protection, but this Ministry had little to do with the formulation and execution of tariff policy—presumably because the tariff was mainly regarded as an instrument for the collection of revenues. Quantitative restrictions came under the direct control of the Ministry of Trade (Department of Exports and Imports) but this Ministry could only recommend changes in tariffs to the Ministry of Finance. The latter remained reluctant to alter tariffs because 'rapid changes in the rates introduce confusion into the tariff law'.[51] Hence it was easier for the Ministry of Trade to protect industry by quantitative restrictions.

Next the Protection Committee always recommended quantitative restrictions. This occurred in part because the Committee found it easier to estimate consumption and output in physical terms, on the basis of actual consumption during the past few years and the capacity of local industry. The Committee would then recommend restrictions on imports to make them just bridge the gap between domestic output and local needs. This the Committee probably found a far easier task than the alternative exercise aimed at finding the correct levels of protective tariffs for particular products. The latter exercise involves a comparison between local and foreign costs of production instead of their prices in the Baghdad market.

Finally the Committee probably shared the official antipathy to the market mechanism and a faith in direct controls. The quotations cited above all neglect relative prices. Domestic demand was measured in physical units and they conceived of demand as price inelastic. On the other hand the foreign supply of goods to compete with local products was thought to be unlimited at prices specially designed by foreigners to destroy Iraq's industry.

But these assumptions are unlikely to be correct and it is unwise to base policy upon them without a proper investigation of each case. While markets in poor countries are far from being perfect, ill-designed Government intervention may often make things worse. In Iraq it was not only the market which was imperfect but the Government administration as well. Supporters of direct controls claimed that when the Government granted import quotas, expressed in value terms, the volume of imports could not be controlled because Iraqi merchants agreed with foreign suppliers to declare false prices on invoices. In other words, the Government administrators were not competent enough to check invoiced prices with prices in countries of origin. Nevertheless, supporters of direct controls expected the same administrors to control domestic prices, protect the interests of industrialists, labourers and consumers by further extension of public control.[52] Early in 1966 the Protection

Committee recommended complete protection for one year of a commodity produced by two firms with the proviso that their activities were watched carefully by the Ministries of Industry and Economy. At the end of a year the Committee reported that it was impossible to show how far the pricing and other policies of this industry were satisfactory because the firms did not supply information and did not send samples of their products to be tested by the Ministry of Industry.[53] This shows how weak was the administration, to say nothing about the undesirability of leaving the choice of samples to the firms themselves instead of the administration.

The consequences of Iraq's policy of protection, which in effect protected any industrial enterprise that existed to whatever extent necessary, were predictable: high costs, high prices and low quality. In 1961, the Central Bank observed that the 'Iraqi consumer has not benefited from the industrial development of the country because Iraq's industrial products are costly and of low quality'.[54] Presumably the argument is that Iraqis will benefit in the long run. The question is how long is the long run? Most of the industries listed in Table VI.3 were established before 1953,[55] and some of them even before the war,[56] but by 1962 they were not only protected by high tariffs but by quantitative restriction as well. The protection policy did not seem to have paid any attention to efficiency; a recent study of industrial productivity in Iraq concluded that 'in the firms studied it was observed that . . . little attention was given to long run policies and cost savings'.[57]

2. Tax Exemptions

Tax exemption is a device which can be used in a variety of forms to encourage private investment in industry, because it leads to a direct increase in the return which a potential investor expects at any assumed level of pre-tax profits. This makes projects profitable for private investors which might otherwise not be undertaken.

Tax exemptions vary in character with the type of taxes. They can be granted for different periods of time and can cover all or only part of the normal tax liability. There are limits in granting tax exemptions, either because the Government may find it difficult to favour industry over other sectors of the economy or because it needs revenue. But if exemptions are too small, for too short a period and are administratively complicated, they have little financial advantage for the potential investor.

The policy of tax exemption in Iraq began with Law No. 14 of 1927 for Encouragement of Industrial Enterprises. This law and its amendments included all basic tax exemptions included in sub-

120   ROLE OF GOVERNMENT IN INDUSTRIALIZATION OF IRAQ

sequent laws promulgated in 1950, 1955, 1961 and 1964.[58] The taxes involved included income tax, stamp duties, tax on property and import duties.

The 1929 law exempted all profits from tax for six years. This was not, however, an important incentive to investment in industry because 'the income tax in itself was very low and tax evasion was the rule before 1939. Then tax rates were increased, the method of collection improved and industrial enterprises were made subject to income tax'.[59] The exemption from income tax was introduced again in 1950 and it continued in subsequent laws. The 1964 law exempted profits not exceeding 10% of the paid up capital of the enterprise for five years (dated from the first year of positive profits), and profits not exceeding 5% of paid up capital for a further five years. The 1964 act is less generous than the 1929 law and more complicated due to the vagueness of terms like 'paid up capital'. But it did exempt undistributed profits needed for improvements and for expansion of the enterprise, provided the sum involved did not exceed 25% of the total profits over a five-year period.[60] This clause assumes that expansion of existing enterprises is more desirable than new investment. The assumption is probably correct since established enterprises usually acquire a level of experience and knowledge of the market which reduces risks of investment within the enterprise and this, presumably, is important in a poor country with a short industrial tradition.

Industrial enterprises were also exempted from stamp duties. Such duties are paid when applications are made to various Government departments or when contracts and other transactions require Government consent. But the rates are extremely low, hence exempting industrial enterprises from these duties was not a significant exemption.[61]

Laws for the Encouragement of Industrial Enterprises exempted these projects from real estate tax for a period of ten years. This exemption involved land, factory buildings and stores, but not administrative buildings. The real estate tax rate was equal to 10% of the annual rental of the property.[62] Moreover the 1964 act included the provision of state owned land at appropriate rentals for a period of 10 years and gave the further privilege of purchasing the land so acquired at prices equal to their market value.

Since 1927, the tariff laws exempted a large variety of machinery and equipment from import duties, the remainder were subject to rates up to 10%, or even more in certain cases. Industrial enterprises covered by the Industrial Encouragement Laws were, however, exempted from these duties.

The profitability of an industrial project can also be improved

OTHER POLICIES TO PROMOTE INDUSTRIALIZATION 121

by exempting imported raw materials from custom duties. Iraq's tariff laws exempted some raw materials from duty and levied moderate or even high duties on others. It has been estimated that the 1955 tariff law has reduced the average duty on these goods from 22% to 15%.[63] From 1930 one of the most important incentives provided for in the industrial encouragement acts was the exemption of raw materials from customs duty. This exemption has been applied within a limited scope in order to avoid misuse by industrial enterprises[64] and to collect revenue for the Treasury. Laws for the encouragement of industry were automatic in operation as far as income tax, real estate tax, stamp duties and import duties on machinery were concerned. Exemptions were granted to firms for defined periods of time provided that they fell within the conditions of the law.[65] But the exemption of raw materials involved Government departments in screening of applications from firms each year.

Whenever a given industrial enterprise requested exemption of raw materials from import duties, officials from the Department for Promotion of Private Industry visited the plant and presented a report to the Industrial Development Committee.[66] In general these reports attempted to measure the firm's imports over the past year and to predict its future consumption. According to the law the amount of raw materials exempted from import duties for the firm is decided in relation to its need for help in the light of the current socio-economic situation of the country.[67] Neither this vague criterion nor the reports are of any help to the Committee. But in the absence of more relevant information and properly defined criteria, exemptions from custom duties were recommended arbitrarily by the Committee and the amount exempted varied from zero to the total of raw material inputs of the firm.

This policy of haphazard exemption gave rise to complaints from both the Federation of Industry which claimed that the amount of raw materials exempted was meagre,[68] and the Ministry of Finance who maintained that it had adversely effected the revenues.[69] The recommendations of the Committee were subject to the approval of the Ministers of Industry and Finance. They usually approved the Committee's recommendations, but the Ministry of Finance exercised a double check on this type of exemption because it had a representative in the Committee—usually the Director General of the Department of Customs and Excise, and because the Minister of Finance could veto the recommendations of the Committee.

Thus Iraq's laws for the encouragement of industry were a screening type of law as far as raw materials were concerned. Theoretically this is superior to the automatic type of law, because it allows

122 ROLE OF GOVERNMENT IN INDUSTRIALIZATION OF IRAQ

the Government to provide exemptions from duties in different degrees to various enterprises according to their desirability. But this type of legislation requires high technical and administrative ability. Appraisal of applications should be efficient, honest and rapid in order to encourage investment.

In the absence of suitably qualified personnel in countries like Iraq tax exemptions should be placed on an automatic rather than a selective basis. One possible technique is to revise the tariff more frequently in order to reduce or eliminate duty on imported raw materials used in large quantities by industrial enterprises. No doubt this would reduce revenue from import duties. But from the point of view of the economy this is almost costless; remission of import duty is not an expense to the Government or a subsidy by the society and if industrialization succeeds it will over the longer run result in a higher level of tax revenue. Yet there is presumably a problem of finding alternative sources of revenue in the short run. Unfortunately not enough relevant information is available to appraise this problem but it is interesting to notice that in 1961 the Ministry of Finance estimated that all tax exemptions extended to the industrial sector amounted to I.D. 2.5 million compared to I.D. 24 million of revenues from import duties,[70] while total Government revenue amounted to I.D. 187 million during the same year; hence even an increase of 100% in tax exemptions on raw materials would have had a marginal effect on Government revenues.

3. *The Licensing of Industrial Enterprises*

Law No. 18 of 1957 made it illegal to establish industrial enterprises with a capital of more than I.D. 20,000 without Government consent. The law stated that licences would not be granted unless investors satisfied the Government that there was sufficient demand for new production. In 1961 the Government extended the system of licensing to include the establishment of any industrial enterprise provided that the cost of machinery and equipment was no less than I.D. 3,000, and the licensing system was extended to include change of location and expansion of industrial enterprises.[71]

The reason for this extension, according to the Ministry of Industry, was that 'one of the principal failures of the previous regime was to leave the establishment of industrial projects to the wishes of private industrialists; this is a dangerous policy because it may lead to the establishment of excess capacity in relation to the domestic market in some lines, while other branches of industry remained unexploited. This means higher average costs and hence higher prices. It follows that Government control is necessary and no

OTHER POLICIES TO PROMOTE INDUSTRIALIZATION 123

licence will be granted prior to an extensive study to make sure that the domestic market needs the extra output'.[72] It is interesting to notice that the only industry of some importance which was claimed to have grown in a capitalistic manner and hence developed wasteful excess capacity was the cement industry which was working at 80% of its capacity during 1958–59. By 1964, however, plans were prepared and it was decided to increase the capacity of this industry significantly for domestic as well as foreign markets.[73]

Applications for licences were made to the Ministry of Industry (Department for the Promotion of Private Industry) and accompanied by the necessary technical and economic data. That department then consulted the Planning Department in the Ministry, the Federation of Industry, the Industrial Bank and other departments. Reports of these departments were then submitted to the Industrial Development Committee and licences were issued by the Minister of Industry on the strength of its recommendations. The criteria used by the Committee in its decisions were:

(1) Did the applicant have sufficient financial resources and contacts with foreign suppliers of industrial machinery?

(2) The importance of the project in relation to demands, the capacity of existing plants and the possible emergence of monopolistic practices.[74]

I have examined all applications for licences submitted during 1965 and the first half of 1966. In most cases the Committee granted a licence because it believed (on the basis of reports from relevant departments) that the domestic market could absorb the additional output. Market demand was estimated from incomplete information on past production and imports, sometimes projected into the immediate future. In no case did officials conduct a proper analysis of costs and prices. Their reports asserted that given projects would provide employment and foreign exchange and never attempted to quantify these claims. Yet once a licence was granted the project became eligible for tax exemptions and other benefits. Moreover the same projects were usually granted whatever degree of protection they required, in order to continue their operations, including a total ban on imports.

This system is bound to foster inefficiency since it tends to encourage the production of any industrial commodity even if it has no long run possibility of competing on international markets. Furthermore, the licensing system, with its attempt to avoid excess capacity, inhibited internal competition. The system was also restrictive and cumbersome. I have already described the procedure in general terms, but to appreciate its complexity let me bring the whole system together at the risk of some repetition. For example, if

124 ROLE OF GOVERNMENT IN INDUSTRIALIZATION OF IRAQ

a textile firm wished to change one of its weaving machines but the productive capacity of the new machine was higher than the old one, the firm had to apply to the Department of Promotion of Private Industry. The application then passed to the Planning Department of the Ministry of Industry; the Industrial Bank and the Federation of Industry were also involved. The reports of these departments were then submitted to the Industrial Development Committee. In cases of conflict a joint committee would be set up to study the problem. The Industrial Development Committee may then recommend that the Minister of Industry grant the licence.

At the second stage the firm would apply to the Ministry of Economy (Department of Imports and Exports), which usually granted the import licence provided that the quota for textile machinery was not exhausted. Even with an import licence the firm still needed authority from the Foreign Exchange Department of the Central Bank.

Even with an efficient administration such complicated and time consuming regulations may well make the firm's relations with the Government the most frustrating barrier it faces. My description of Iraq's administration in Chapter II suggests that the Government administration was far from efficient. During 1965–66 when I was an administrator in the Ministry of Industry I was told by numerous industrialists who eventually received licences, that had they been aware of the bureaucratic complications they would never have committed themselves to the investment. One wonders how much investment never begins because of maladministration?

REFERENCES

1. Federation of Industry, *Year Book*, 1957–58, p. 221; and Government of Iraq, *Iraqi Revolution, One Year of Progress*, p. 59
2. Ministry of Industry, *Annual Report*, 1961, p. 50
3. Kemp, *The Mill-Bastable Infant Industry Dogma*, pp. 65–7
4. Corden, *The Calculation of the Cost of Protection*, pp. 36–8
5. Johnson, *The Costs of Protection and Self-sufficiency*, p. 371
6. Chenery, *Comparative Advantage and Development Policy*, pp. 20–5
7. Meier, *International Trade and Development*, p. 132
8. Jamil, *Commercial Policy of Iraq*, p. 49
9. Hassan, *Economic Development of Iraq*, pp. 345, 349
10. Jamil, *Commercial Policy of Iraq*, pp. 51–54
11. *Ibid.*, pp. 54, 174, 194
12. Central Bank of Iraq, *Annual Report*, 1956, p. 22 and Hassan, *Economic Development of Iraq*, pp. 355, 360
13. Law No. 31 of 1962
14. Jamil, *Commercial Policy of Iraq*, pp. 68, 72, 221, 402 and National Bank of Iraq, *Annual Report*, 1950, p. 54
15. Table VI.1, column 9
16. See Table VI.1

OTHER POLICIES TO PROMOTE INDUSTRIALIZATION   125

17. Central Bank of Iraq, *Bulletin, New Series*, No. 4, 1967, p. 25
18. These rates of course protect local industries but they are obviously higher than rates required for protection alone
19. Jamil, *Commercial Policy of Iraq*, p. 424
20. Jamil, *op. cit.*, pp. 62, 208; Hassan, *Economic Development of Iraq*, p. 353 and Table VI.2
21. al-Nasrawi, *Financing Economic Development in Iraq*, p. 138
22. Table VI.5, column 8
23. See Table VI.2
24. Walter, *The European Common Market*, p. 52
25. *Ibid.*, p. 54
26. Law No. 30, 1962
27. Haberler, *Some Problems in the Pure Theory of International Trade*, p. 238
28. Cordon, *The Tariff*, pp. 195–7
29. Jamil, *Commercial Policy of Iraq*, p. 486
30. al-Jalili, *Lectures on Economics of Iraq*, p. 68
31. Central Bank of Iraq, *Annual Report*, 1961, p. 43
32. Government of Iraq, *The Iraqi Revolution, One Year of Progress*, p. 59, and *The Iraqi Revolution in its Second Year*, p. 144
33. National Bank of Iraq, *Annual Report*, 1953, p. 17 and Federation of Industry *Annual Book*, 1957–58, p. 224
34. Hassan, *Economic Development of Iraq*, pp. 370–1, Federation of Industry, *Annual Book*, 1957–58, pp. 221–30
35. Only in 1965 was the value of licences issued less than the value of imports but in that year the value of licences did not include imports of the public sector. Central Bureau of Statistics *Statistical Abstract*, 1965, p. 236
36. Central Bank of Iraq, *Annual Report*, 1965, p. 125
37. Iraqi Federation of Industry, *Year Book*, 1957–58, pp. 224–5 and Hassan, *Economic Development of Iraq*, p. 370
38. Ministry of Industry, *Annual Reports*, 1960, p. 51 and 1961, p. 63
39. Kindleberger, *International Economics*, pp. 251–3
40. Maldistribution of import licences in Iraq has been referred to by al-Habeeb, *Notes on Commercial Policy of Iraq*, p. 17 and Explanatory Note to Law No. 30, 1962, p. 29
41. Ministry of Industry, *The Position of the Industrial Sector of Iraq*, p. 42
42. Government of Iraq, *Iraqi Revolution, One Year of Progress*, pp. 35, 56
43. Mr. al-Shamma, Assistant Director General in the Ministry of Industry and its representative in the Committee
44. The name of the Ministry of Trade was changed to Ministry of Economy, in 1963
45. I have read (14) of these reports published in Federation of Industry, *Quarterly Magazine*, for the period 1962–65
46. National Bank of Iraq, *Annual Report*, 1954, p. 30
47. Ministry of Industry, *Annual Report*, 1961, p. 7
48. Government of Iraq, *The Iraqi Revolution in its Second Year*, the Report of the Ministry of Trade, p. 144
49. Adams, *Iraq's People and Resources*, p. 126 and Langley, *The Industrialization of Iraq*, p. 253
50. Government of Iraq, Law No. 30, 1962, The 9th amendment of Tariff Law No. 77, 1955. The Explanatory Note, p. 28
51. *Ibid.*, p. 29
52. Hassan, *Economic Development of Iraq*, p. 369
53. Ministry of Economy, Permanent Committee for Protection, *Report No. 77 of 1967*, p. 2

126   ROLE OF GOVERNMENT IN INDUSTRIALIZATION OF IRAQ

54. Central Bank of Iraq, *Annual Report*, 1961, p. 44
55. Ministry of Economy, *Industrial Census*, 1954, pp. 10–11
56. Langley, *Industrialization of Iraq*, pp. 58–9
57. Suleiman, *Industrial Productivity in Iraq with Special Reference to Selected firms*, 1953–63, p. 297
58. Laws No. 43, 1950, No. 72 of 1955, No. 31 of 1961 and No. 164 of 1964
59. Jamil, *The Commercial Policy of Iraq*, p. 288
60. Short periods of tax exemption will have meagre results if the income tax is too high to ensure adequate returns for risk and management after the conclusion of tax holidays. This could occur if investors have to pay high personal income taxes on distributed dividends as well as taxes on company profits. In this respect Iraq's Income Tax Law No. 178 of 1959 and amendments imposed heavy taxes. Thus the tax imposed on residents commences at a low rate of 3% on income up to I.D. 500 and then increases up to 90% on incomes above I.D. 20,000 per year. The rates levied on industrial enterprises starts from 10% on profits up to I.D. 1,000 and increases to 45% on income above I.D. 13,000. But when tax rates are so high few projects will offer a high enough profit before taxation to give an attractive return after tax unless they are able to charge the public high monopolistic prices
61. Jamil, *The Commercial Policy of Iraq*, p. 185
62. Laws No. 162 of 1959, No. 35, 1927 and No. 17 of 1940
63. Hassan, *Economic Development of Iraq*, p. 361
64. Jamil, *The Commercial Policy of Iraq*, p. 579
65. According to 1964 law, enterprises eligible for these privileges must carry out their main process on machinery whose total value must be at least I.D. 3,000, supplemented by at least 60% Iraqi capital and employ no more than 10% of non-Iraqi unskilled labour
66. This Committee is attached to the Ministry of Industry, its members represent the Ministries of Industry, Finance, Planning and Economy, Federation of Industry and an expert. Article 2 Law No. 164 of 1964
67. Law No. 164 of 1964 article 10
68. Iraqi Federation of Industry, *Quarterly Magazine*, March 1965, pp. 23–5 and Speech by the Chairman of the Federation in the same issue p. 12
69. Ministry of Finance, *Note on the 1962 Budget*, p. 6
70. *Ibid.*, p. 6
71. Law No. 31 of 1961
72. Ministry of Industry, *Annual Report*, 1960, p. 58
73. Hassan, *Studies in Economics of Iraq*, p. 129 and Ministry of Industry *The Position of the Industrial Sector*, pp. 51–2
74. Ministry of Industry, Laws and Regulations, pp. 163, 172–3

Chapter VII

SUMMARY AND CONCLUSIONS

From 1921 the Iraqi Government has played an active role in the economic development of the country. Up to 1950 it devoted an average of 12% of its annual resources to capital formation and its share in gross capital formation was approximately 34%. The Government invested mainly in social overhead capital but its financial resources were not enough to promote rapid expansion and by the early 'fifties Iraq's infra-structure remained underdeveloped. Given the obvious need for social overhead investment and the small budget surplus available to it, the Government could not feasibly implement a policy of industrialization based on direct public investment. But in the early 1950s when oil revenues increased enormously it became possible for it to increase investment in all sectors of the economy.

Nevertheless, a subsidiary cause of the relatively slow rate of public capital formation before 1950 can be found in the lack of continuity in the formulation and implementation of development programmes engendered by political instability. Between 1921–50 the Cabinet changed about every eight months and each new Government attempted to revise the economic policy of its predecessor. Since political instability continued to afflict Iraqi politics into the 'fifties the Government in power in early 1950 saw that it was essential to devise an institutional framework which could protect the state's effort to promote economic development from the consequences of frequent Cabinet changes.

Thus in 1950 the Government established an autonomous agency called the Development Board to formulate and implement investment programmes. The majority of the Board came from outside the Government and were appointed for five years. The Board received a substantial part of the oil revenues paid to the Iraqi Government. It employed its own personnel and set up an organization free from the rigidities of normal civil service regulations. But its autonomy was short-lived and in 1953 the administrative machinery of the Board was transferred to a new Ministry for Development. The Board remained in operation with the Minister of Development as a member; the majority of its members were not

128 ROLE OF GOVERNMENT IN INDUSTRIALIZATION OF IRAQ

politicians. Although the dangers of political instability came back in 1953 the Board managed to maintain a substantial degree of autonomy and this brought a large element of continuity into development policy.

After the Revolution of 1958 the Development Board was abolished and a new Planning Board created which consisted entirely of Ministers. In 1964 full time executive members were added to the Planning Board but the majority of its members continued to be departmental Ministers. Under the new organization, the implementation of plans became the responsibility of Government departments but the departments could not expand their personnel and raise their capacity to implement plans without approval from the Ministry of Finance. This situation created serious bottlenecks due mainly to lack of co-ordination between the Ministries.

In the post 1958 period the formulation and implementation of the Government's industrial programmes were the responsibility of the Ministry of Industry. This Ministry included administrative units responsible for almost all aspects of industrialization such as planning, design, construction, technical and economic research, manpower and market surveys. In practice the design of projects, feasibility studies, the training of labour and the construction of industrial projects were carried out by private agencies, and the functions of the administration were confined to the supervisory tasks previously undertaken by the far simpler technical section of the Development Board's organization for industry.

One weakness of the Development Board's organization lay in its excessive centralization—i.e. its failure to delegate detailed planning and administration to subordinate agencies and other Government departments. After the Revolution of 1958 the Government attempted to decentralize and it made the Planning Board responsible for general planning and entrusted other departments with the task of detailed planning and implementation. In practice the Planning Board became preoccupied with detailed planning and problems of implementation and it never gave enough attention to basic policy issues such as the assessment of total resources, the selection of alternative patterns of investment, etc. Nor did it give serious consideration to the improvement of the administration, which remained the most important obstacle to Iraq's economic development.

Between 1951 and 1958 the Development Board formulated three investment programmes and from 1959–65 the Planning Board formulated another three. The Development Board simply sought to invest 70% of Iraq's oil revenues in various sectors of the economy. It did not set out to achieve target growth rates of production and

SUMMARY AND CONCLUSIONS 129

income for different sectors of the economy. The Planning Board's approach was to set target rates of growth for economic sectors which in turn determined the required rates of investment and saving. After the Revolution of 1958 the Government reduced the share of oil revenues devoted to capital formation from 70% to 50%, while the programmes of the Planning Board required resources equivalent to almost all available oil revenues.

With given financial resources, the Development Board decided on the scale and timing of investment in each sector of the economy on the basis of reports prepared for it by professional economists and other advisors, but it used simple common sense rather than mathematical models to avoid inconsistencies in its plans. The Planning Board tried to prepare more sophisticated investment programmes but its plans turned out to be similar, at least in form, to those formulated by the Development Board. Both Boards decided on the basic issues of resource allocation on the basis of a general attitude towards the economic development of Iraq and of reports by private consultants on different sectors.

Nevertheless, the Development Board emphasized agriculture, while the Planning Board gave priority to industry. Any general discussion of priorities is bound to be inconclusive, but it does seem that the Development Board's bias towards agriculture reflected the correct priority for the economic development of Iraq in 1950–65. The majority of the population remained in the countryside and continued to depend on agriculture for their livelihood. There were, moreover, excellent opportunities for the development of agriculture while the country lacked the variety of raw materials, skills and markets essential for the rapid development of a viable industrial sector. The current 1970–74 plan, however, gives first priority to agriculture and devoted 34.4% of the planned investment of the Central Government to agriculture compared to 24.5% for industry.[1]

The funds available for investment always exceeded the amounts required for the execution of existing feasible and well-prepared projects. If there had been more of these projects, a proper assessment of their costs and benefits could have offered a more satisfactory solution to the problem of resource allocation. Moreover, the scarcity of well-designed projects was again due mainly to the weakness of the administration, particularly the shortage of qualified specialists capable of designing and appraising projects.

While the formulation of consistent plans is important, their actual implementation determines the growth of production and income. Implementation can be measured by comparing plan targets with actual achievements. Apart from the sixth plan (1965–69) and the current 1970–74 plan, the Iraqi plans do not contain proper

130 ROLE OF GOVERNMENT IN INDUSTRIALIZATION OF IRAQ

overall or sectoral targets for production, income, employment or for saving foreign exchange. One can only measure plan implementation in terms of investment targets. Throughout 1951–65 expenditure on capital formation was substantially less than planned investment. But while the gap between planned and actual investment narrowed under the management of the Development Board (1951–58), it widened under the Planning Board (1959–65). Throughout the period the achievement of investment targets was lower for industry than for any other sector, and the gap between actual and planned industrial investment increased during 1959–65. Fulfilment of targets for the industrial sector, however, increased from 47% in 1965 to 72% in 1966, but declined sharply to 47% in 1967 and to only 24% in 1968, which was again lower than in any other sector.[2]

During 1951–65 there was a marked deviation of the actual pattern of investment from the planned pattern. The extent of deviation again increased under the management of the Planning Board. Thus the implementation process upset the priorities of the Planning Board to a greater extent than those of the Development Board.

The country's inability to invest available funds in sound projects, the large and increasing gap between targets and achievements, and the distortion of established priorities during the implementation of plans, resulted from a complex combination of administrative inefficiency, ambitious plans and political factors.

Thus for five of the six plans covering the period 1951–65, planners exaggerated the amount of funds that the Government was prepared to devote to capital formation. But even if all the funds made available by the state had been invested, actual capital expenditure would have amounted to only 63% of planned investment. The Planning Board assumed that it would receive 50% of oil revenues and that the remainder of finance required would come from other Government sources. This procedure not only obscured the failure of the Government to allocate more than 50% of oil revenues for development but it also helped to distort the priorities of the plans for the allocation of investible funds.

Plan implementation depended on the efficiency of Iraq's public administration, which suffered from excessive centralization, low morale, lack of co-ordination and a weak sense of urgency. Promotion was based on seniority, officials were frequently shifted from one position to another regardless of experience and quality. Few remained in one department long enough to become really expert. There were also serious defects in administrative procedures. After the Revolution of 1958 Government current expenditure increased rapidly but most of it went to departments like defence which had little direct connection with the capacity of the administration to

SUMMARY AND CONCLUSIONS 131

implement plans, and the result was a regrettable decline in the ratio of capital expenditure to total Government expenditure from 39.8% in 1958 to 24.9% in 1965 and 23.6% in 1967.[3]

The ratio of actual to planned expenditure was lowest for the industrial sector and this reflected the relative weakness of the Ministry of Industry. This was partly due to the reorganization of 1959, which placed the machinery for implementation under the control of the Ministry of Finance. Although the Planning Board gave high priority to industry in the allocation of investible funds, the Ministry of Finance did not allow a parallel increment in the size of the administration dealing with industry. There is no doubt that other factors beside expenditure affect the capacity of an administration to implement plans (the internal organization of each ministry, quality of its staff, the relative complexity of the field of work, etc.). But it was probably necessary to increase the personnel of the Ministry of Industry considerably in order to render it capable of investing all the funds allocated to capital formation in the industrial sector. In other words the Planning Board formulated investment programmes without proper consideration of the capacity of the Ministry of Industry to implement them. Would it not have been more sensible for the Planning Board to gear its industrial plan to the administrative capacity of the Ministry of Industry and to demonstrate administrative bottlenecks? At least this might have persuaded the Ministry of Finance to do something about it.

According to Law No. 90 of 1970 the Departments concerned with plan formulation and implementation in the Ministry of Industry were amalgamated into a new Department called General Organization for Industrial Design and Construction. Such a semi-autonomous organization can assume more freedom of action and is usually less rigidly controlled by the Ministry of Finance, but as yet we have no experience of its working to permit appraisal.

The Central Bank of Iraq was established to facilitate the supply of credit to all sectors of the economy but it failed to appreciate the needs of industry, and never encouraged commercial banks to extend short term loans to manufacturers. Furthermore, by confining its discount facilities to short term bills of exchange and promissory notes of three months' maturity it positively discouraged them from supplying long term credit to industry.

The Industrial Bank sought to encourage industrialization through the provision of long and short term credit by way of participation in the equity capital of industrial companies, through the provision of technical assistance and by preparing feasibility studies of industrial projects. Although the Bank accomplished use-

132 ROLE OF GOVERNMENT IN INDUSTRIALIZATION OF IRAQ

ful work in most of these fields, up to 1950 when its capital was increased, it was handicapped by the shortage of funds. Recently the financial resources of the Bank have declined because the Government has failed to increase its paid up capital and because a large part of its funds were locked up in industrial enterprises which were nationalized. Although the Planning Board never utilized all the investible funds made available to it, the Board failed to appreciate the role of the Industrial Bank and refused to increase the Banks' capital despite continuous requests to do so.

Planners have declared recently that they will support the Bank to enable it to encourage further private and mixed industrial enterprises.[4] But so far the only practical measure taken by planners has been to devote 10% of the net profits of the Bank before taxes to the Central Government's Plan Budget.[5]

Because commercial banks failed to meet industrial demands for short term credit, the Industrial Bank has devoted some of its resources to short term loans. Moreover, recently the Bank has started to reallocate its assets towards short term securities. It would, however, have been better for the Bank to concentrate on the provision of long term loans and for the Central Bank to have encouraged commercial banks to meet industry's needs for short term credit, because the Industrial Bank was the only financial institution which provided long term industrial credit, because commercial banks were less likely to be persuaded to advance long term loans, and because all resources of the Industrial Bank could have been utilized for the provision of longer term loans. At the beginning of 1970 new measures were taken by the Bank to check the growth of short term loans and these loans were extended mainly to new enterprises.

Up to 1965 the Bank participated in the equity capital of 21 enterprises but until 1964 it refrained from holding a majority of shares. Recently it has changed its policy in order to exercise control over companies in the mixed (private and public) sector of industry. But since investors lack confidence in enterprises controlled by public organizations, if the Bank really wants to attract private capital and initiative into the mixed sector, it would be more sensible for the Bank to go back to the old policy.

The Bank also provided technical assistance and prepared feasibility studies for medium and small scale industrial projects. But its activity in this field has not been satisfactory basically because of a shortage of qualified personnel capable of undertaking technical and economic studies.

The Government also promoted the growth of Iraqi industry by protecting it from foreign competition. Originally the tariff was de-

SUMMARY AND CONCLUSIONS 133

signed to obtain revenue, but gradually the Government used it to encourage domestic industry by levying low duties on imported inputs and high rates on commodities which competed with domestic industry. Nevertheless, up to 1965 the tariff remained the single most important source of revenue apart from oil revenues. In general, duties were kept at moderate levels in order to permit a limited volume of imports to compete with domestic industry and to provide revenue for the Treasury. The Government fixed these rates haphazardly, which can be seen in the extremely wide variation in Iraqi custom duties levied for protective purposes only. Thus in 1962 duties varied from 17% to 170%, a range which could not be expected to reflect differences in efficiency of industries considered 'infants'.

Tariffs were supplemented by quotas and import prohibitions. Whenever the productive capacity of a domestic industry was thought to be sufficient for local needs the Government banned imports entirely. When local demand was estimated to be greater than available capacity the Government established a quota to bridge the gap. But the official investigation into these questions did not take into account any consideration of long run efficiency. The Government made no attempt to compare domestic costs of production of an industry with real costs for the economy, or to ascertain whether the protected industry had any possibility of becoming efficient. It attached little value to competition and saw no disadvantages in local monopolies.

The Government also utilized tax exemptions to encourage private investment in industry. The exemptions involved income taxes, stamp duties, real estate taxes and import duties. Apart from the latter all tax exemptions were automatic in operation. For example, profits not exceeding 10% of paid up capital were exempted from income tax for five years and this exemption was granted to all industrial firms which fell within the scope of the law. But the exemption of raw materials from import duties involved Government departments in screening applications from every industrial firm each year. Theoretically this might be thought superior to automatic forms of tax exemption because it enabled the Government to operate a selective policy. But the administration was simply not competent enough to appraise these applications efficiently and made arbitrary decisions. The result was continuous complaints of partiality by industrialists. It would have been preferable to set up this exemption on an automatic basis. Alternatively tariff rates could have been revised more frequently to reduce duties or eliminate them on raw materials consumed in large quantities by industrial enterprises.

K

134 ROLE OF GOVERNMENT IN INDUSTRIALIZATION OF IRAQ

The Government attempted to control the allocation of private investment in order to avoid excess capacity. Licences were granted for the establishment of new enterprises and the expansion of old ones whenever the Government thought that the domestic market could absorb additional output. Market demand was estimated on the basis of incomplete information about consumption and no proper analysis of costs and prices was conducted before licences were granted. In fact, the system encouraged the production of any industrial commodity regardless of long run efficiency. Furthermore, the administration of the system was restrictive and cumbersome. It involved several departments, none of which was capable of conducting cost benefit analysis efficiently and rapidly. Once again the policy makers overestimated the capacity of the administration and imposed on it duties far beyond its capacity.

Different public agencies were concerned with the industrialization of Iraq. Thus tariff policy, investment programmes, quantitative import restrictions, monetary policy and tax exemption were each dealt with by a separate body and the Government failed to co-ordinate their albeit limited efforts into a comprehensive policy.

REFERENCES

1. Ministry of Guidance, Law No. 70 for 1970, *The National Development Plan for the Financial Years 1970–74*, pp. 9, 131 (in Arabic)
2. Central Bank of Iraq, *Bulletin, New Series*, No. 2, 1968, p. 29 and No. 4, 1969, p. 29
3. See Table IV.8 and Central Bank of Iraq, *Bulletin, New Series*, No. 4, 1969, p. 15
4. Ministry of Guidance, *The National Development Plan, 1970–74*, p. 134
5. *Ibid.* p. 3

BIBLIOGRAPHY

Abu-El-Haj, R., 'Capital Formation in Iraq 1921–57', *Economic Development and Cultural Change*, Vol. IX, No. 4, Part 1, July 1961, pp. 604–617, reprinted in *Quarterly Magazine of the Iraqi Federation of Industry*, December 1963, pp. 1–8.

Adams, D., *Iraq's People and Resources*, California Publication in Economics, Vol. 18 (University of California Press, Berkeley, 1958).

al-Atraqchi, M. A., *Statistical Analysis of the Pattern of Merchandise Foreign Trade of Iraq 1948–62*. Unpublished Ph.D. Thesis, University of London, 1965.

al-Atrash, M. H. F., *Monetary Policy in an Underdeveloped Economy, with special reference to the Experience of Egypt, Iraq and Syria, 1951–58*. Unpublished Ph.D. Thesis, University of London, 1962.

Asseily, A. E., *A Central Bank for Lebanon*. Ph.D. Thesis, University of London, 1966. (Revised version, published by Khayat Book and Publishing Co., Beirut, 1967.)

Buchanan, N., *International Investment and Domestic Welfare* (Holt, New York, 1946).

Cameron, R., *Banking in Early Stages of Industrialization, A Study in Comparative Economic History* (Oxford University Press, New York, 1967).

Carmody, A. T., 'The Level of the Australian Tariff, A Study in Methods', *Yorkshire Bulletin of Economic and Social Research*, Vol. 4, No. 1, January 1952, pp. 51–65.

Central Bank of Iraq (called National Bank of Iraq up to 1956), *Annual Reports*, 1950–65.

Central Bank of Iraq, *Quarterly Bulletin*, 1950–66.

Central Bank of Iraq, *Bulletin, New Series*, No. 1, 1965, Nos. 1, 2, 3, 4, 1967.

Central Bank of Iraq, *Laws, Regulations and Ordinances* (Government Press, Baghdad, 1965).

Chenery, H., 'Comparative Advantage and Economic Policy', *American Economic Review*, Vol. LI, No. 1, March 1961, pp. 18–51.

Chenery, H., 'Pattern of Industrial Growth', *American Economic Review*, Vol. L, No. 4, September 1960, pp. 624–654.

Chenery, H., 'The Application of Investment Criteria', *Quarterly Journal of Economics*, Vol. LXVII, No. 1, February 1953, pp. 76–96.

Clark, C., *Conditions of Economic Progress*, third edition (Macmillan, London, 1957).

Clark, V., *Compulsory Education in Iraq*, UNESCO, 1951.

Corden, W. M., 'The Calculation of the Cost of Protection', *Economic Record*, Vol. XXXIII, No. 64, April 1957, pp. 29–51.

Corden, W. M., 'The Tariff', in Hunter, A. (ed.), *The Economics of Australian Industry, Studies in Environment and Structure* (Melbourne University Press, Parkville, 1963), pp. 174–214.

al-Dally, A., 'Problems of Industrial Enterprises in Iraq', American University of Beirut, *Middle East Economic Papers*, 1954, pp. 37–54.

Federation of Iraqi Industry, *Year Book*, 1957–58 (al-Rabita Press, Baghdad, 1958, in Arabic).

Federation of Iraqi Industry, *Quarterly Magazine*, 1962–65 (in Arabic).

136   BIBLIOGRAPHY

Fenelon, K. G., *Iraq, National Income and Expenditure* (al-Rabita Press, Baghdad, 1958).

Galenson, W., and Leibenstein, H., 'Investment Criteria, Productivity, and Economic Development', *Quarterly Journal of Economics*, Vol. LXIX, No. 3, August 1955, pp. 343–370.

Government of Iraq, Development Board, *Development of the Tigris–Euphrates Valley*, Summary of Report by Knappen-Tippetts Abbett-McArthy, Engineers of New York (al-Ani Press, Baghdad, 1954).

Government of Iraq, Development Board, *Compilation of Laws, Concerning the Development Board* (Revised), (Government Press, Baghdad, 1952).

Government of Iraq, Development Board and Ministry of Development, *Law No. 43 of 1955 for the Projects of the Development Board* (Government Press, Baghdad, 1955, in Arabic).

Government of Iraq, Development Board and Ministry of Development, *Law No. 54 of 1956 for the Amendment of Law No. 43 of 1955* (Government Press, Baghdad, 1956, in Arabic).

Government of Iraq, Development Board and Ministry of Development, *Second Development Week* (Beirut, printed 1957).

Government of Iraq, 14th July, Celebration Committee, *The Iraqi Revolution, One Year of Progress and Achievement* (Government Press, Baghdad, 1959).

Government of Iraq, Higher Committee for the Celebration of the 14th July, *The Iraqi Revolution in its Second Year* (Government Press, Baghdad, 1960).

Government of Iraq, Ministry of Economy, Principal Bureau of Statistics, *Statistical Abstracts*, 1951–57.

Government of Iraq, Ministry of Economy, Principal Bureau of Statistics, *Report on the Industrial Census of Iraq, 1954* (al-Nur Press, Baghdad, 1956).

Government of Iraq, Ministry of Economy, The Permanent Committee for Protection, *Report No. 77 of 1967*, mimeographed (in Arabic).

Government of Iraq, Ministry of Education, *Report on Education for the Year 1949–50* (in Arabic).

Government of Iraq, Ministry of Finance, Directorate General of Budget, *Explanatory Note on the 1962 Budget* (Government Press, Baghdad, 1962, in Arabic).

Government of Iraq, Ministry of Finance, Directorate General of Accounts, *Annnal Reports on the Accounts of the Republic of Iraq, 1957–63*, (in Arabic).

Government of Iraq, Ministry of Finance, Directorate General of Accounts, *Report on the Accounts of the Development Board for the Fiscal Year 1959* (Government Press, Baghdad, 1960, in Arabic).

Government of Iraq, Ministry of Guidance, *Law No. 181 of 1959 for the Provisional Economic Plan, 1959–62*.

Government of Iraq, Ministry of Guidance, *Law No. 70, of 1961, for the Five-Year Detailed Plan 1961–65*.

Government of Iraq, Ministry of Guidance, *Law No. 87 of 1965, for the Five-Year Economic Plan 1965–69* (in Arabic).

Government of Iraq, Ministry of Industry, *The Feasibility Study of the Nassiriah Woollen Textile Project*, Baghdad, 1966. Mimeographed.

Government of Iraq, Ministry of Industry, *The Position of Industry in Iraq*, A Study Presented to the Conference on Industrial Development in the Arab Countries, held in Kuwait on March 1966 (al-Aadhami Press, Baghdad, 1965, in Arabic).

Government of Iraq, Ministry of Industry, *Annual Reports*, 1961, 1962 and 1964 (in Arabic).

Government of Iraq, Ministry of Industry, *Compilation of Laws and Regulations Concerning Industry* (Government Press, Baghdad, 1964, in Arabic).

BIBLIOGRAPHY

Government of Iraq, Ministry of Planning, Central Bureau of Statistics, *Summary of Iraq Foreign Trade Statistics 1927–60* (Government Press, Baghdad, 1961).

Government of Iraq, Ministry of Planning, *Report on the Draft Broadlines for the Detailed Economic Plan*, Baghdad, November 1960. Mimeographed.

Government of Iraq, Ministry of Planning, *The Five-Year Economic Plan, 1965–69*, Baghdad, 1966. Mimeographed (in Arabic).

Government of Iraq, Ministry of Planning, Central Bureau of Statistics, *Quarterly Bulletin*, No. 2, 1966.

Government of Iraq, Ministry of Planning, Central Bureau of Statistics, *The Industrial Census of Iraq, 1962* (Government Press, Baghdad, 1964, in Arabic).

Government of Iraq, Ministry of Planning, Central Bureau of Statistics, *Statistical Abstract, 1958–65*.

Great Britain, Colonial Office, *Special Report to the Council of the League of Nations on the Progress of Iraq During the Period, 1920–31* (H.M.S.O., London, 1931).

Hanson, A. H., *The Process of Planning, A Study of India's Five-Year Plans* (Oxford University Press, London, 1966).

Hashim, J. M., *Capital Formation in Iraq 1957–62*. Unpublished Ph.D. Thesis, University of London, 1966.

Hassan, M. S., *Studies in Economics of Iraq* (Talia House Publications, Beirut, 1966, in Arabic).

Hassan, M. S., *Economic Development of Iraq, Foreign Trade and Economic Development 1958–1964*, (Asriah Library Publications, Beirut, 1965, in Arabic).

Hasseb, K., *The National Income of Iraq, 1953–63*, The Central Bank of Iraq, 1964. Mimeographed.

Industrial Bank of Iraq, *Annual Reports*, 1950–65 (in Arabic).

Industrial Bank of Iraq, *Profit and Loss Accounts for the Years 1951 and 1952*.

Industrial Bank of Iraq, *The Industrial Bank, A Report Published on May 1962 and March 1965*. Mimeographed.

Industrial Bank of Iraq, *Notes on the Framework of the Five-Year Economic Plan*, February 1965. Mimeographed (in Arabic).

International Bank for Reconstruction and Development, *The Economic Development of Iraq* (The Johns Hopkins Press, Baltimore, 1952).

International Bank for Reconstruction and Development, International Development Association, *Current Economic Position and Prospects of Iraq*, September 1963. Mimeographed.

International Monetary Fund, *International Financial Statistics*, Vol. XXI, No. 6, June 1968.

Ionides, M., *Divide and Lose, the Arab Revolt, 1955–58* (Geoffrey Bles, London, 1960).

Iraq Petroleum Company, Oil Information and Statistics Section, *A Report on Operation of Oil Companies in Iraq: Summary of Annual Statistics*, 12th April, 1966. Mimeographed.

Iversen, K., *A Report on the Monetary Policy of Iraq*, National Bank of Iraq, 1954.

Jalal, F., *The Implementation Time Path of the Rayon Project in Iraq, A Case Study*, Report Presented to the Inter-Regional Working Party on Training of Economic Administrators, Organized by the United Nations and O.E.C.E., held in Paris on September 1965. Mimeographed.

al-Jalili, A., *Lectures on Economics of Iraq* (al-Risalah Press, Cairo, 1955, in Arabic).

Jamil, M. H., *Commercial Policy of Iraq* (Nahdat Misr Press, Cairo, 1949, in Arabic).

138   BIBLIOGRAPHY

Johnson, H., 'The cost of Protection and Self Sufficiency', *Quarterly Journal of Economics*, Vol. LXXIX, No. 3, August 1965, pp. 356–372.

Kahn, A., 'Investment Criteria in Development Programmes', *Quarterly Journal of Economics*, Vol. LXVII, No. 1, February 1953, pp. 38–61.

Kanaan, T. H., *Input–Output and Social Accounts of Iraq, 1960–63*, Ministry of Planning, Baghdad, 1966. Mimeographed.

Khadduri, M., *Independent Iraq, 1932–58*, 2nd edition (Oxford University Press, Oxford, 1960).

al-Khalaf, J. M., *The Economic, Physical and Human Geography of Iraq*, third edition (Dar al-Marifah, Cairo, 1965, in Arabic).

Kemp, M. C., 'The Mill—Bastable Infant Industry Dogma', *Journal of Political Economy*, Vol. LXVIII, No. 1, February 1960, pp. 65–7.

Kindleberger, C., *International Economics* (Irwin, Illinois, 3rd ed., 1963).

Langley, K., *Industrialization of Iraq* (Harvard University Press, Cambridge, Massachusetts, 1961).

Lewis, W. A., *Principles of Economic Planning* (Allen and Unwin, London, 1952).

Little, Arthur, D., Inc., *A Plan for Industrial Development in Iraq*, A Report Jointly Sponsored by the Development Board of Iraq and the U.S.A. Operation Mission in Iraq (Cambridge, 42, Massachusetts, 1956).

Longrigg, S. H., *Iraq 1900–1950, A Political Social and Economic History* (Oxford University Press, Oxford, 1953).

al-Nasrawi, A., *Financing Economic Development in Iraq: the Role of Oil in a Middle Eastern Economy* (Praeger, New York, 1967).

Nevin, E., *Capital Funds in Underdeveloped Countries* (Macmillan, London, 1961).

Polack, J., 'Balance of Payments Problems of Countries Reconstructing with Help of Foreign Loans', *Quarterly Journal of Economics*, Vol. LVII, No. 2, February 1943, pp. 208–240.

al-Qaisi, F., *Iraq's Banking System after Nationalization*, A Lecture Presented to the Iraqi Economic Association, Baghdad, 1967. Mimeographed (in Arabic).

Qubain, F. I., *The Reconstruction of Iraq, 1950–57* (Atlantic Books, London, 1958).

Reddaway, W. B., 'Importance of Time Lag for Economic Planning', *Economic Weekly*, Vol. XII, Nos. 4, 5, 6, January 1960.

Riggs, F. W., *Administration in Developing Countries, The Theory of Prismatic Society* (Houghton Mifflin, Boston, 1964).

Salter, Lord, *The Development of Iraq: A Plan of Action* (Iraq Development Board, Baghdad, 1955).

Sayers, R. S., *Central Banking After Bagehot* (Clarendon Press, Oxford, 1957).

Sen, A. C., 'On Optimizing the Rate of Saving', *Economic Journal*, Vol. LXXI, No. 283, September 1961, pp. 479–495.

Suleiman, H. A., *Industrial Productivity in Iraq with special reference to Selected Firms 1953–63*. Unpublished Ph.D. Thesis, University of London, 1967.

Tinbergen, J., *Central Planning, Studies in Comparative Economics* (Yale University Press, New Haven, 1964).

Tinbergen, J., 'The Relevance of Theoretical Criteria in Selection of Investment Plans', in M.I.T., *Investment Criteria and Economic Growth* (Asia Publishing House, London, 1961).

United Nations, Centre for Industrial Development and Economic and Social Office in Beirut, *Industrial Planning Programming and Policies in Selected Countries of the Middle East*. Report presented to the Conference on Industrial Development in the Arab Countries, held in Kuwait on March 1966. Mimeographed.

United Nations, Centre for Industrial Development and Economic and Social Office in Beirut, *Financing of Manufacturing Industry in Selected Countries of*

BIBLIOGRAPHY

the Middle East, Report presented to the Conference on Industrial Development in the Arab Countries, held in Kuwait on March 1966. Mimeographed.

United Nations, Department of Economic and Social Affairs, Statistical Office, *National Income and Per Capita Income of Seventy Countries*, New York, 1951.

United Nations, Department of Economic and Social Affairs, *A Handbook of Public Administration, Current Concepts and Practices, with special reference to Developing Countries*, New York, 1961.

United Nations, Department of Economic and Social Affairs, *A Study of Industrial Growth*, New York, 1963.

United Nations, Department of Economic and Social Affairs, *Process and Problems of Industrialization in Underdeveloped Countries*, New York, 1955.

Viner, J., Stability and Progress: The Poorer Countries' Problems, in Hague edited, *Stability and Progress in the World Economy* (Macmillan, London, 1958), pp. 41–65.

Walter, I., *The European Common Market, Growth and Pattern of Trade and Production* (Praeger, New York, 1967).

Waterson, A., *Development Planning, Lessons of Experience* (Oxford University Press, London, 1966).

INDEX

Adams, D. 28, 117
Agriculture 3, 9, 41, 68, 47–50, 129
   and industry 50–2
Agricultural-Industrial Bank 6, 88–9

Balance of payments 10, 102, 112
British Mandate 1–3
Buchanan, N. 52

Capital formation 3–7, 14, 127
Central Bank—See under financial
   institutions
Chemical industry 36, 40
Chenery, H. 52, 54, 56
Commercial banks—See under finan-
   cial institutions
Council of Ministers 20

Department for Promotion of Private
   Industry 121, 123–4
Development, Ministry of 17, 19, 37,
   78, 128
Development Board—See under plan-
   ning institutions
Development problems—See under
   Iraq

Education 2, 8, 27–8

Fenelon, K. G. 7
Financial institutions
   Central Bank 20, 84, 86–8, 94–5, 117,
     119, 131–2
   Commercial banks, 80–8, 132
     and industrial credit 81–6, 94
   Industrial Bank 33, 84, 86, 88–100,
     123, 131–2
     Loans of 91–6
     and the Ministry of Industry
      95–6
     Participation in industry 96–9
     Resources of 89–91
     Technical assistance, 99–100
   Ministry of Finance 3, 75, 77, 91,
     118, 121, 122, 128, 131

Galenson, W. 52
General Organisation for Industrial
   Design and Construction 131
Government Oil Refinery Administra-
   tion 33

Health 2, 8

IBRD missions 7, 8, 9, 14, 27, 28, 29
   33, 48, 53, 99
Industrial Bank—See under financial
   institutions
Industrial Credit—See under financial
   institutions and industrialization
Industrial Development Committee
   121–3
Industrialization 21, 22, 50, 54–7
   Compared with agriculture 50–2
   and the Industrial sector in Iraq 4,
     9, 39, 41, 46, 50–1, 73–5, 94,
     102–26
   and the infant industry argument
     103–4
   and relations with the financial
     sector 80–101
Industry, Ministry of 19, 21–7, 71, 77,
     92, 100, 102. 113, 117, 119, 121,
     128
   Composition of 22–4, 131
   and the Industrial Bank 95–6
   and Laws for Industrial Encourage-
     ment 111, 119–22
   and Licensing 122–4, 134
   and tax exemptions 119–22, 133
Iraq
   Conditions in 1920 1–3
   Conditions in 1950 7–10
   National income 6
   Problems of development 10–12
Iraqi Government
   Administration 27–9, 71, 130–1
   Development efforts 1921–50 3–7
   July 1958 Revolution 71, 78, 98, 111,
     115, 128, 130

INDEX

Iraqi Government—*cont.*
Political problems 11–12, 20, 78–9
Revenue and expenditure 3–7, 10, 14–31, 105, 122

Kanaan, T. H. 49
Khan, A. 52
Kirkuk Oil Fields, 33, 36

Leibenstein, H. 52
Lewis, W. A. 59
Licensing—See under Ministry of Industry
Little, A.D., Inc. 25, 36, 38, 39, 48, 53, 78, 84
Longrigg, S. H. 12

Ministries—See under relevant heading
Mosul 33, 41

Nevin, E. 88

Oil 10–11, 14, 15, 35, 43, 46, 78, 102, 105, 127, 130
Ottoman rule 1–3

Planning
Implementation 62–79, 130–1
Organisation and administration 12, 17–18, 22–6, 71–8—See also planning institutions
Project appraisal 52–4, 57–9
Sectoral allocation 44–53, 62, 64–9, 72
Size of plans 42–4
Planning Board—See under planning institutions
Planning institutions
Department of Industrial Planning 22, 24–7
Development Board 14–19, 20, 43–4, 53, 64, 78, 127–8
Differences from Planning Board —See Planning Board
Emphasis on agriculture 47–50, 129
Function of 16
Plans of 32–8
Procedure 18–19, 25–6, 71–8
Ministry of Planning 19, 21, 44, 46, 71, 77

Planning Board 19–21, 41, 43, 68, 91, 128
Administration 71–8, 131
Attitudes of 50–2
and Department of Industrial Planning, 24–7
Differences from Development Board 21, 45–6, 68–9, 128–30
Plans 38–42
Plans
1st plan 1951–58 33–4
2nd plan 1955–59 35–7
3rd plan 1955–60 37–8, 78
4th plan 1959–62 38–9, 68
5th plan 1961–65 39–41, 68
6th plan 1965–69 41–2, 50, 54, 57, 81, 129
Polack, J. 52
Port of Basrah Authority 4, 8
Private sector 46, 102–26
Public building sector 68, 70, 75

Qaiyara Bitumen Refinery 33

Rafidian Bank 80
Reddaway, W. B. 62

Salter, Lord 17, 28, 37, 48, 49
Sayers, R. S. 88
Social overhead capital 2, 4, 6–8, 40, 127
Soviet Union 39, 78
and 1959 agreement with Iraq 24, 39, 57, 68
Suez crisis 63, 69

Tax exemptions—See under Ministry of Industry
Trade, Ministry of 115, 117–18
and the Permanent Committee for Protection 115–19
and protection—See trade protection
Trade protection 102–19, 132–3
Quotas 111–19
Tariffs 104–11, 120–1

United Nations 78, 100

Viner, J. 49

Willcocks, W. 3